MAP
OF THE
SOUL:
SHADOW
OUR HIDDEN SELF

MURRAY STEIN
in collaboration with
Steven Buser, Leonard Cruz
and Sarah L. Stein

CHIRON PUBLICATIONS • ASHEVILLE, N.C.

www.ChironPublications.com

Interior design by Danijela Mijailovic
Cover design by Claudia Sperl
Printed primarily in the United States of America.

ISBN 978-1-63051-800-4 paperback
ISBN 978-1-63051-801-1 hardcover
ISBN 978-1-63051-802-8 electronic
ISBN 978-1-63051-803-5 limited edition paperback

Library of Congress Cataloging-in-Publication Data

Names: Stein, Murray, 1943- author.
Title: Map of the soul - shadow : our hidden self / Murray Stein.
Description: Asheville : Chiron Publications, 2020. | Series: Map of the soul; volume 2 | Includes bibliographical references. | Summary: "In this second book in the series, Map of the Soul - Shadow: Our Hidden Self, Dr. Murray Stein explores the dark recesses of our psyche, as well as the shadow images in BTS' latest songs in their album Map of the Soul: 7. The Korean Pop band, BTS, has been taking the world by storm with a series of albums inspired from Dr. Stein's concepts titled Map of the Soul. Dr. Stein has joined them in expressing these same Jungian themes in a companion book series. The landscape of the soul has many contours and some hidden regions. This book speaks about obscure, typically unacknowledged aspects of the psyche. The shadow may appear initially like an unwanted intruder but those who become acquainted with their shadow discover it to be a vast storehouse of treasures and resources on the journey of self-discovery. Whereas the persona is the part of your personality that is revealed to others, the shadow is the part of your personality that is concealed from others and ourselves. The shadow often declares itself through sudden, often brutal reversals. At the collective level, the shadow proves capable of magnetizing people in the same direction, often with very destructive results. The person intent on living a more full, authentic life will be well served by becoming acquainted with the shadow. The author and collaborators are deeply indebted to BTS, whose world-wide popularity points to their remarkable ability to tap into universal themes that dwell in the collective domain. BTS' music inspired this work and we hope this work will inspire others to explore the deep recesses of their inner life"— Provided by publisher.
Identifiers: LCCN 2020016251 (print) | LCCN 2020016252 (ebook) | ISBN 9781630518004 (paperback) | ISBN 9781630518011 (hardcover) | ISBN 9781630518028 (ebook)
Subjects: LCSH: Shadow (Psychoanalysis) | Self.
Classification: LCC BF175.5.S55 S84 2020 (print) | LCC BF175.5.S55 (ebook) | DDC 155.2—dc23
LC record available at https://lccn.loc.gov/2020016251
LC ebook record available at https://lccn.loc.gov/2020016252

To BTS and their
ARMY of fans

Special thanks to *BTS ARMY,*
Carla Postma-Slabbekoorn
at the ARMY Help Center,
Laura London at Speaking of Jung
and to *BTS* for bringing Jungian
psychology to a new generation.

Table of Contents

Introduction
By Murray Stein

In the physical world, the word "shadow" is defined as the absence of light behind an object that is facing a light source like the sun. In psychology, however, this word has a different meaning. If the *persona* is the part of your personality that is revealed to others around you, the *shadow* is the part of your personality that is concealed from them and even from yourself. It is a mistake, however, to think that the psychic "shadow" is nothing but the absence of the light of consciousness in a certain area of the soul. It is more than that. It is substantial, and it is active.

In psychology, *shadow* is a term that refers to hidden motives and attitudes. Shadow motives have an energy and a goal of their own, which are usually very different from the adapted and conformist motives of the *persona*. The motives are guided by unconscious attitudes, which are psychological constellations like biases and prejudices. The *shadow* side of the personality may be as dramatically different from the usually manifest personality as we find in the novel *Strange Case of Dr Jekyll and Mr Hyde* by Robert Louis Stevenson. The novel depicts a split personality, one of which is benign and adapted and the other criminal and psychopathic. It is a portrait of good and evil housed in a single person and alternately active in the world. The *shadow* is as powerful as the *persona* in this case.

And the *shadow* is complex, because it is made up not only of one but a collection of motives that serve an underlying attitude. Usually, these are motives that a person would not want others to see, so they are conveniently kept out of sight and unacknowledged. They are motives like envy and greed and cold selfishness. They work by subtle insinuation and manipulation, seeking to destroy and undermine others in order to claim superiority for oneself. Often, they are successfully hidden from sight because the *persona* shines its bright light in the face of others who are observing the person and receiving the treatment. They are often so well concealed and disguised that even the person who exercises them does not fully know when they are active. And sometimes they are hidden in plain sight because the *persona* is so powerful and distracting that people are blinded to what is happening right in front of them. We don't want to bring such motives into the light and focus on them because when they are revealed, they cause embarrassment and shame. Shame is the typical emotional reaction when a person is confronted by others with their *shadow* enactments or wishes, unless, that is, they are sociopaths or psychopaths, in which case they try another deceptive cover-up.

The *shadow* lies at the fringe of consciousness, just at or beyond the edge of consciousness and more or less out of easy sight except to the trained eye. To catch the *shadow* at work, we have to train ourselves to look at the fringe of our awareness and to observe our hidden thoughts and motives. It's not an easy thing to do, and we have a natural aversion to spotting the *shadow* in ourselves. Besides that, the fringe of consciousness trails off into the darkness of deep unconsciousness, and the further the *shadow* lies in that territory the harder it is to spot. It's like trying to see a dark object against a dark background. It's nearly invisible.

Shadow-spotting is something we like to do to other people. This is called gossiping. When we point to the bad traits in other people and tell other people how awful they are, we are shadow-spotting. We might be seeing what is there, or we might be seeing our own disowned *shadow* that is being unconsciously pro-jected onto another person. When we say they are "mean" or "selfish" or "greedy," we may be projecting our own similar qualities. It's very natural to project unconscious *shadow* traits and motives onto other people. Spotting the *shadow* in others is a tricky business, and we should be careful when we play that game. We may be revealing aspects of our own *shadow*.

A Japanese acquaintance of mine recently told me a story from her past that sharply depicts this dynamic of *shadow* projection. When she was a teenager, she spent a year studying in an American high school as an exchange student. As it happened and not too surprisingly, she was the only Japanese person in the school. The student body was divided into two distinct groups based on race, and there was often tension between them, as is pretty often the case in such situations. The less socially favored students felt badly treated by the more privileged ones, and there was mutual *shadow* projection going on between them on a regular basis. Unfortunately, the year the Japanese student was in this school was also a significant anniversary of the Japanese surprise attack on Pearl Harbor that initiated America's entry into the Second World War, so the whole student body was made aware of the "bad Japanese" who had attacked the "innocent Americans." This created a strong bond between the two groups and among all the Americans because they could all identify with the victims of this nefarious sneak attack. And what made this bond even stronger among them was that together they could turn on the Japanese student as one of the bad aggressive people who had attacked "our country." The Japanese student felt this hostile, aggressive energy coming at her especially strongly from the young men in the less privileged group, who would call her names in the hallway and harass her on her way home after school. Here you can see how the *shadow* piece of the psyche—aggression and racism—was directed against the innocent Japanese girl. She became what we call a "scapegoat." This is a person who collects *shadow* projections from a whole group of people and is usually so badly bullied that she is forced to leave the group.

In this case, however, the scapegoat was rescued by an empathic school counselor who explained to her what was happening. The counselor's intervention was successful because she used her own experience to explain the psychology of *shadow* projection. She came from the same underprivileged racial group as these male students did, and she told the Japanese girl about how it was for her growing up in a rural community where she had experienced daily taunts and harassment from the other students in her school because of her racial difference. The Japanese student could then feel that in the school counselor she had a friend who understood her painful situation. As a result of this helpful insight into the psychology of *shadow* projection, the Japanese student decided to study psychology, and when she returned to Japan and entered the university, this was the subject she chose as her major. Today she is a school psychologist and a professor of clinical psychology in a Japanese university. The experience of receiving the projection of *shadow* and the importance of understanding how it works put her on a whole new and meaningful course in life. This is what we sometimes call making lemonade out of the lemons life delivers to us. Some of our most important and transformative experiences in life come from painful shadow-filled moments like this.

Becoming aware of your personal *shadow* is usually not a pleasant experience, but it is the path to deeper areas of the psyche and thus essential for wholeness. Without integration of the *shadow* into the conscious household, something essential is lacking. *Shadow* integration is also the key to assuming responsibility for your actions and therefore constitutes an important contribution to the community and the world. Jung once wrote: "One does not become enlightened by imagining figures of light, but by making the darkness conscious."

The same principle applies to nations. Nations, too, have their *shadows* in the form of cultural biases and nationalistic selfishness. These are the dirty secrets in a nation's history, and sometimes the *shadow* enactments of nations are extreme, and their crippling effects pass down through through later generations. Only if they are acknowledged and made conscious can a nation recover its full identity and move forward in its cultural evolution. Nations must accept responsibility for their actions if they are to continue to grow and mature, just as individuals must. *Shadow* work is required on many levels. Just as Germany, for instance, has had to look at its past actions during the Nazi period of its history, and as the United States must look at its aggressions in various parts of the world on behalf of its selfish economic and political interests, so nations across the globe must delve into these shadowy areas of history and politics if their citizens are to be freed from the consequences of *shadow* enactments. The ancient notion of "karma" speaks to this insight. Today we speak of "transgenerational transmission of trauma" (TTT), and we can also speak of "transgenerational transmission of responsibility" (TTR), which might be called social karma.

The chapters in this little book are intended to help the reader become more aware of the many manifestations of the psyche's *shadow*, individually and collectively. Becoming conscious of the *shadow* and taking responsibility for its manifestations open the way to the next level of psychological development, which has to do with making contact with the *anima* and *animus*, the links to the center of the self. Our discussion of this level will be left for a further volume in this Series on the Map of the Soul.

Chapter 1
BTS' *Interlude: Shadow* - A Psychological Reflection

By Murray Stein

This chapter is adapted from an interview of Murray Stein conducted by Laura London on the podcast Speaking of Jung: Interviews with Jungian Analysts episode #53.

As I write this, BTS has just released a 3-minute video of the song Interlude: *Shadow*, which will appear in its new album, **Map of the Soul: 7**. It is sung solo by BTS member Suga. The video images communicate intense emotion, which matches the feeling tone of a confrontation with the *shadow*. Whenever we touch *shadow* material in ourselves or others, emotion rushes in. Throughout the song *Interlude: Shadow*, we feel this emotional intensity in Suga's songs of passionate desires for fame, power, and fortune and of his fear and anxiety. We also see it in what is happening around him: In the background, threatening *shadow* figures lurk and threaten to overwhelm him.

Throughout the video, there are images of shattering glass and mirrors. Confronting the *shadow* is bound to be a *shattering* experience. It destroys one's self-images and the constructed images of the surrounding world. It breaks our self-confidence and destroys our naiveté. This can, of course, prepare the ground for a new consciousness, but in the meantime it's a harrowing experience.

What is the *shadow*? It's a carefully concealed part of the psyche that clings to the backside of the *ego*. It sits there in obscurity, moving quietly and unobtrusively in the background as we go about our daily affairs. Some parts of the *shadow* lie just on the fringe of consciousness. We can sense them occasionally out of the corner of the eye. But mostly the *shadow* is not apparent to the *ego*, which is focused elsewhere and looking straight ahead. But then sometimes we stop and take a look within and see that behind our *persona* there lurks a figure, which we speak of darkly as the *shadow*.

If we are courageous, we can admit it into consciousness. We can let it speak, and then we can catch aspects of it lying there at the fringe. When Suga sings, as though to himself and somewhat brutally, "I want to be a rap star, I want to be the top, I want to be a rockstar, I want it all mine ...," this is what he is doing. He is letting the *shadow* speak through him, and it's showing its usually hidden and secret features. In these words, Suga is telling us, his listeners-in, about some of his most passionate wishes and desires. It's as though he is speaking to himself in private and letting us listen in on his internal dialogue.

The hidden part of ourselves that we call the *shadow* is our coldest egotism, our most profoundly selfish part. When we face it, this can be a truly shattering experience.

The *ego* in itself is nothing more and nothing less than the center of our consciousness. It is the "I" that observes, whether ourselves or the world around. It also acts, sometimes on conscious intentions but often out of unconscious motivations. In the latter case, the *ego* doesn't really know why it's doing something in particular and not something else. And sometimes it is taken over by powerful emotions and big ideas that have their source in the unconscious. In that case, the *ego* becomes possessed by them and enacts their desires and intentions. It loses its neutrality and becomes another personality. This is the case when the *shadow* takes control. The *ego* becomes identified with the *shadow* for a period of time. It leaves the nice *persona* behind and speaks with the voice and intentions of the *shadow*. This is what we hear in the words Suga is singing.

Of course, we have the capacity to love as well as to hate, a capacity for altruism and a capacity for selfishness. BTS sings frequently and beautifully about love: being in love, being with love, loving ourselves, and loving those around us. But in this album, BTS is singing about the dark side, the *shadow*. The *shadow* is the other side of love. It houses our greed and ambition and lust for power over others, as Suga sings so well. Whereas love reaches out to others and wants their good, the *shadow* withdraws into egotism and wants to use others for its own benefit and to control them for selfish purposes. Our *ego* can lean either way. It can be taken up by the light or by the dark.

The *shadow*, it must be noted, is not limited to individuals. It also takes up residence in groups, tribes, nations—in all types of collectives. You can find the *shadow* at work powerfully in politics and economics. Wherever power is an issue, there the *shadow* lurks and finds opportunity to unleash its ice-cold forces. The *shadow* is noticeably active in the interactions between nations, and when they engage in war, they typically project their own darkest *shadow* impulses and intentions onto the enemy. The other nation is all evil and bad while the homeland is totally noble and righteous. God is on our side; the Devil is behind theirs! *Shadow* activation splits and polarizes the world into good and evil parts.

For some people, the whole world is seen as controlled by evil powers and owned by the *shadow*. Various religious groups have declared the world to be created by an Evil Demon, and they have isolated themselves from it as much as possible. They declare themselves to be pure and the world to be polluted. This makes the world itself into a scapegoat for their *shadow* projections.

But in psychological reality, the *shadow* is a part of all of us, individually and collectively. This is one of the main realizations in the song *Interlude: Shadow*. It is a recognition that the *shadow* is an inherent part of ourselves, even though we struggle to disown it.

The *persona*, which BTS sang about in the previous album, **Map of the Soul: Persona**, presents the individual as a socially acceptable being. When the *ego* speaks "in the *persona*," it's speaking in an image that is socially adapted and adjusted. When the *ego* is in a *shadow* position, however, or gets taken over by the *shadow*, it's not in a socially acceptable position. When a person is speaking or acting out of the *shadow*, people will turn away and criticize them for their impolite or socially incorrect attitudes. Some people, however, will be drawn toward them and quietly or secretly support them if their own *shadow* parts resonate there. This happens when *shadow* politicians appear on the scene. An accumulation of *shadow* energies will gather around these figures, and they can become politically very powerful because they symbolize the *shadow* that's resident in the collective psyche. The people who don't support them and are able to see the *shadow* for what it is will stay away or fight it in order to keep it from dominating the collective world. In the polling booth, when people are alone, they can act out their *shadow* impulses and vote for the *shadow*-bearing politician, and the pollsters will be surprised by the outcome because so few people confessed to supporting the *shadow* politician openly.

Many people are fascinated by *shadow* figures even if they are also at the same time frightened by them. Criminals and outlaws draw a lot of attention. They attract people's interest because they represent a part of emotional life that ordinarily remains under cover. When you go to a movie like "Joker," which features a shocking *shadow* figure, you can participate vicariously in their *shadow* behavior and enactments. It's a way of experiencing and releasing *shadow* energies in a fairly safe way, unless the film gives permission to start acting and behaving in the ways that the *shadow* character in the film does. But for most people, it's a kind of release. It lets a little of the steam out of the repressed unconscious. We try to be good so much of the time that our *shadow* can build up a great deal of tension, which needs to be released somehow. "It's unhealthy to be too good," Jung once declared. He was speaking as a psychiatrist, not as a teacher of morals. It's because if you keep the *shadow* too repressed, it will cause psychological damage to yourself and to others around you because it will be projected onto them. You can develop a neurosis, and inner conflicts can develop that make life very painful. Psychotherapy tries to find ways to release some of this energy. A basic rule in psychotherapy is that you can speak "in the shadow" without getting criticized or condemned for it. Gradually, some of these *shadow* energies can be somewhat integrated into consciousness and accepted. Then the *shadow* is not so bottled up inside. Anyway, some of the *shadow's* energy can be very useful for the *ego's* functioning in the world.

It's very similar with regard to aggressive sports. American football, for instance, can be very rough and often borders on sheer brutality. For the fan, this is a welcome release for that bottled-up energy. The fans live their *shadow* aggression vicariously through the players. The games have rules, so it's not like all-out warfare. Warfare lets the *shadow* run wild, fully on the loose. There are some rules of war, but they are often not observed in the heat of combat. "Total war," which is what Hitler practiced, means no rules and nothing held back. Here, the *archetypal Shadow* has the last say on everything.

Interlude: Shadow is about becoming conscious of some features of the *shadow* in an honest and straightforward way. In this song, Suga becomes aware of *shadow* motives and desires, and he dialogues with them. In the last part of the piece, there's a conversation between the *shadow* and Suga. The *shadow* speaks to him and tells him that they are one and that they can never be separated. Dialogue was also how Jung engaged the *shadow* in his famous *Red Book*.

There we can read his dialogues with all sorts of light and dark figures, including the Devil himself. This is a way of becoming familiar with those parts of the self. By imaging them and entering into a conversational relationship with them, a person allows them not only to become more familiar but also drains some of the energy out of them. By bringing them into a conscious relationship with the *ego*, there is a change in the relations between the opposites, and they become a set of polarities. When there are stark opposites, there is no gray zone, there is no bridge between the black and the white—there are only total winners and total losers. If the opposites can be changed into polarities, they have a dynamic movement between them, like the pair yin and yang in Chinese philosophy. They can work against each other, they can work with each other, but they don't split apart into opposites.

The value of inner dialogue is self-knowledge, and this helps a person to avoid the splitting that is so prevalent when the *shadow* is totally repressed.

Turning back to the music video *Interlude: Shadow*, the sequence of movements begins with Suga emerging from a door with a bright red surround. Red is the color of very strong emotional energy, the color of passion, sometimes of anger, sometimes of lust. We don't know what is behind the door, but I imagine it's a house of darkness. He is coming out into consciousness and is going to reveal what he knows. He is alone. Down the hallway are a number of men also standing alone in front of other doors, each one isolated and showing no relationship to the others. Suga will be the solo performer in this song. It's all about the isolated individual, alone, outside of relationship to the others who happen to be around him. Suga stands for the BTS group's *shadow*, isolated from the world around. This is a mark of *shadow* existence.

Suga sings, "I wanna be rich, I wanna be the king, I want it all mine, I wanna be me, I want a big thing, I want it all mine ..." This is the *shadow* of greed speaking through the *ego*. And then, suddenly, he has a moment of recognition of his dangerous situation, and he falls into terrible anxiety. Now he suddenly experiences the harsh reality of the opposites: intense light begets intense darkness. The brighter the light, the darker the dark. The higher he rises above everyone, the farther is the ground below him. Suga fears falling, which is the inevitable result of overreaching and flying too high too fast. He sings: "The moment I'm flying high as I wished, my *shadow* grows in that blasting stark light. Please don't let me shine. Don't let me down. Don't let me fly. Now I'm afraid." He's praying for deliverance from the consequences of his *shadow* enactments. He's speaking for BTS. Success breeds anxiety. The richer you become, the more you fear poverty.

Many people fear the consequences of too much success gained too soon. It's an instinctual fear, and it makes sense. Success breeds envy in others, and in their envy, they will plot the demise of the favored one. Just think of Iago in Shakespeare's masterpiece of evil, *Othello*. Or recall the famous cautionary tale from Greek mythology, the story of Icarus. Icarus and his father, Daedalus, were trapped in a labyrinth. Daedalus, a skilled craftsman, builds them each a set of wings so they can fly out. The father ascends to a moderate height and lands safely outside. Icarus, on the other hand, becomes thrilled with his power to fly. He flaps his wings too hard and flies too high, whereupon the sun melts the wax holding his wings to his naked arms, and he crashes to his death. The fear of flying too high too fast is not a bad thing. It's a useful anxiety. We have these anxieties for a reason.

Toward the end of the song we hear a voice singing: "I'm you, you're me, now do you know? Yeah you are me, I'm you, now you do know." Who is singing these words? It's Sugo's alter *ego*, his *shadow*. The song has shifted from monologue to dialogue. His *shadow* is speaking to him, and it's telling him a truth. It is the *shadow* speaking to Suga saying, "We are one, do you get it? You can't get rid of me. We are connected. We will always be together. We are one body, and we are going to clash, we are me ... do you know this?" This forecasts a new consciousness and an acceptance of the *shadow*. The *shadow* will always be there, and it's better to accept this truth than to deny it and try to repress the *shadow*.

What we see in this song is the picture of ambition and success. It's a message that says when you're in the world and working hard, you want to rise. But ambition also activates the *shadow* side of *ego* striving upward. One makes decisions that are selfish in a hidden way, perhaps putting slyly yourself ahead of somebody else, or stabbing them quietly in the back, or doing things that are not quite correct or even illegal or unethical. We do these things semi-consciously or totally unconsciously. One can't avoid it. The song of Suga shows a deep recognition that we can't get away from the *shadow*. Nobody is free of the *shadow*. This is the interior, introverted side to the *shadow*.

There is also an extroverted side to *shadow*. We project our personal and the collective *shadow* onto the marginalized people in society, onto criminals, refugees, immigrants and people of a different nationality or race. They are the shadow-bearers of society. And this projection denies the deep bond of kinship that actually exists among all of us as human beings. Suga ends his song with: "We are one body and we are gonna clash. We are you, we are me, this do you know?" He is affirming our commonality and ultimate oneness. We are all related.

Chapter 2
Further Reflections on the Lyrics of BTS' *Map of the Soul: 7*

This chapter is adapted from an interview with Murray Stein conducted by Laura London on the podcast Speaking of Jung: Interviews with Jungian Analysts Episode #55.

It is widely accepted that BTS's concept of *Map of the Soul* is based off Dr. Stein's writings. This chapter analyzes many of the lyrics in *Map of the Soul: 7* from Dr. Stein's experience as a Jungian analyst. While not all of the tracks on the album are discussed in this particular chapter, Dr. Stein has discussed the first five tracks in his earlier book *Map of the Soul: Persona* and further reviews songs on the ego in his book *Map of the Soul: Ego*.

BTS and the Number 7

It was somewhat of a surprise when BTS titled the current album *Map of the Soul: 7*. Many of us were expecting them to continue along the lines of their last release, *Map of the Soul: Persona*, and proceed with either *Map of the Soul: Shadow* or *Map of the Soul: Ego*. *Map of the Soul: 7* was both creative and unexpected.

BTS choosing the number 7 can be looked at in a number of ways. The obvious elements are the 7 members of the band and that they've been together for 7 years. But the number 7 is extremely important in symbolic representations as well. For instance, we have 7 days of the week. That's not an accident. In the biblical text, God created the world in 6 days and rested on the 7th. The number 7 completes things. It is a number that brings us to a sense that something is finished, something is done, and we can now take a rest. One can think about it in a number of different ways, but I think in reference to this album it seems to indicate they are finished with something. They are finished with a phase, at least. They have done their work, and now they are going to take a rest.

7 as a Prime Number

7 is a prime number, and prime numbers are only divisible by one and themselves. So 7 is an indivisible unit. BTS is a single entity, unbreakable. They are a prime number, and they've worked hard to get there. They live together, they spend practically all their waking hours together, they identify strongly with the same ideas, music, style of living, etc. In a sense, the BTS is a single personality made up of seven moving parts. Of course, you

wonder how long this can go on before they have to live their own separate individual lives. The day is coming when this unit will have to break apart or break down and reformulate as another kind of unit, perhaps more complex, with more individual features to the personalities in the group. But they've worked very hard to form a prime singularity as a group and now they are celebrating it even as they are anticipating a different future.

The Seven Numbers in the Individuation Process

In Jungian Psychology, the number 7 is often associated with the alchemist Maria Prophetissa. Maria Prophetissa is a legendary early alchemist in the first centuries of the Common Era. She describes a formula, sometimes referred to as the *Axiom of Maria Prophetissa* stating: "One becomes two, two becomes three, and out of the three comes the one as the fourth." And when you add the three to the four, of course, you get 7.

Each of the numbers from One to Seven has a psychological meaning. "One" is the first and original state of consciousness, the beginning. It is what Jung called the *Pleroma*. "All is One"—there is no differentiation or separateness in this state. It is the original state of wholeness that we come into the world with at birth. This contains the whole potential for the personality that has yet to be realized in time and space.

"Two" results when there is the first differentiation in consciousness. Where there was One before, now there are Two. This is consciousness of a distinction between self and other. This is an advance of consciousness, seen developmentally: The child discovers the difference between itself and others. Consciousness is beginning to do its work of making distinctions, and this continues as a sense of individual identity grows stronger. This also shows the division between consciousness and the unconscious. Consciousness is emerging from the waters of the unconscious and creating a perception of the differentiated world of objects, outer and inner.

Out of the interaction of these two elements in the psyche a third function emerges: cognitive thinking and imagination. "Three" represents the possibility for abstract thinking and planning. This is the birth of the Spirit and is responsible for culture. Language becomes a tool for thinking and communicating, and with this come abstract possibilities like the naming of groups and imagining things that do not exist. Three means consciousness of possibilities that hover above the earth; it is rich with ideals, abstract values, and possibilities for future development.

Now the fourth element is needed. When Four appears in the formula, it means that the ideas, ideals and possibilities created in the Three become grounded in reality and actualized. The Four is often associated with the feminine and with the Earth. The movement from Three to Four represents a movement toward the grounding of projects in time and space: The city gets founded, the academic degree is achieved, the business is set up and begins functioning.

The number Five represents the "*quinta essentia*," the essential core of the personality. The achievement of the Five is to discover this essential core of the Self and to relate to it consciously.

The number Six represents the union of opposites, masculine and feminine. Consciousness and the unconscious are united. Jung called this the *mysterium coniunctionis*, and his last extensive book bears this title.

After that we arrive at the number Seven, a holy number, a number of transcendence and ultimate completion of a journey begun with the number One. In the Bible, the seventh day is the day of rest, and it arrives after the previous six days of development, differentiation, and creation of consciousness. This is shown in the image of a *triangle placed in a square*, the Three within the Four. This Seven represents the sense of spiritual completion. This is the individuated personality.

The movement from One to Seven represents the individuation process.

Behind the Persona of BTS

In their album *Map of the Soul: 7*, BTS is breaking out of the stereotypical persona of the successful K-pop boy's band and revealing their deeper nature to us. Although many of their fans might not see it, BTS has suffered and struggled. They've worked extraordinarily hard to get to where they are, and they've suffered along the way. They've had their ups and downs, yet people likely don't see that. All they see is the bright lights of the entertainment on stage— the beautiful smiles, the colorful hair, the clothes, the acrobatic dancing. But in this album, BTS is saying, "We're human beings behind this entertainment facade. It's a mask. We're real people, we have a history, and we have struggles, we've suffered." This message comes through in this album loud and clear.

Beyond the suffering, however, there's also a theme of resilience, of overcoming their problems and setbacks. Ultimately, it's a very affirming album. It reveals the suffering and the reality behind the persona, but it also affirms and speaks to the resilience of the group. The song *We Are Bulletproof: The Eternal* is sung to their ARMY. They have been tremendously supported by their fans. They've survived and come through, and they're singing about it. The album is celebratory as well as revealing a lot of pain and agony.

BTS, Rebirth and Transformation

All of us go through phases of transition and transformation in our lives. While that is particularly true in childhood, it continues throughout our life span. Carl Jung described this as the individuation process. There are several critical developmental periods. The transformation during adolescence, from childhood to adulthood, is the most obvious. Again at midlife, there's a transformation from early adulthood to mature adulthood, and then late in life there's another transformation into old age. These are death and rebirth experiences, death in the sense that the old identity dies and rebirth in the sense that a new identity is born.

We have to shed our old identities, the way the snake sheds its skin. As the snake grows, the skin become too small for it and needs to shed. We also outgrow our form sometimes, like when our baby teeth fall out. People often dream of losing their teeth, and that's a part of the growth process. They're losing their old concepts, their old way of digesting their experiences, and they're going to have to wait a while until new teeth grow in place. Just as we experience this on a physical level, the psyche also goes through its processes of shedding the old skin when the old identity doesn't fit the new reality anymore. People experience this in relationships. For a while a relationship feels just perfect, but then it becomes tedious and perhaps worn out. People then feel they've outgrown the relationship. They might divorce and go their separate ways or stay together but somehow transform the relationship. Other people find themselves stuck in a worn-out career and go in a new direction. The old skin doesn't fit anymore. We have to let go of the old identity in order to become the new person that we are going to be for the future.

A group does this as well. Groups go through death and rebirth processes. You can see that in history with empires and nations and religious organizations. Over time, they go through periods of ascendancy and they peak. Then they decline and perhaps die away. Often they're reborn into a new version of themselves. I think BTS is anticipating this as a group. They are reaching a peak and are foreseeing a transformation and a rebirth process. Yet, this is going to be quite challenging.

I wrote a book some years ago called *In Midlife*. It's about three stages within the transformation process that we call midlife: death, liminality and reintegration. Death is the letting go of the old life that is no longer working. Next is an uncomfortable period called liminality. It is full of uncertainty, facing the unknown, and discovering new aspects of our personality. Finally, reintegration brings a new sense of self to move forward with. It can take a lot of time. The midlife transformation is often five to 10 years long. Now that BTS members have hit incredible heights within their career, they must begin anticipating the trials of transformation. *Map of the Soul: 7* suggests this anticipation.

THE SONGS IN *MAP OF THE SOUL: 7*
Tracks 1 through 5 were previously reviewed in Dr. Stein's book *Map of the Soul: Persona*.

Track 6: *Interlude: Shadow*
– See separate chapter on *Interlude: Shadow* in this book

Track 7: *Black Swan*
**- This song is reviewed more thoroughly in Book 3
in the series, *Map of the Soul: Ego*.**

Track 8: *Filter*

Filter is Jimin's solo song, and he asks, "Which of me do you want?" BTS is an entertainment group, and they can cheer you up, excite you or calm you down. This filter idea is "I can be anything you want, just tell me what you want, I'll be it." It's not the way relationships work in the long run, but it's a phase perhaps, and it's certainly what entertainment tries to do. For a period of time, it will make you feel something outside your normal frame of reference. BTS is saying, "We can do that. We can dance for you. We can help you." They're great entertainers and engage with the audience extraordinarily well.

It can also be speaking of a bias toward one of the 7 in the group. Which one of the 7 are we perhaps more drawn to? "Which of me do you want?" could also mean which one of BTS do you want? It could be the member you're attracted to the most or the one you can identify with the most. It could also be the one you project a part of yourself onto the most and thus feel closest to.

You have 7 BTS members moving around, and it's hard to keep them apart unless you focus on one or two. One of the functions of consciousness is to differentiate. So, when you see a group, you begin trying to separate them and distinguish them. This one does this better, that one does that better. I like this one better than that one. It's a normal part of conscious functioning to do that. So that's how we develop one-sidedness and bias, by making selections and preferences. I like RM because he speaks English and I can understand him better, and he made such a good talk at the United Nations. So, I would tend to favor him, but I'm also drawn to the group as a whole.

Track 9: *My Time*

In *My Time*, Jungkook sings, "It feels as if I became an adult quicker than anyone, and there are traces of what I missed. Am I living this right?" He mentions how his friends are on a subway while he's in an airplane. It's something that one hears from a lot of celebrities who became famous when they were young. They feel as if they've missed out on their childhood and adolescence. The BTS members were enlisted at a pretty early age into the group. Their lives became intense and very fast moving and highly disciplined, and they missed out on a lot of normal teenage experiences. It's as if they're put in a chute or a tunnel, and they're shot through and don't see what's outside that framework. So, when they're 25, as they are now, and they look back, they see how narrow that tunnel was and think of all the experiences that they missed.

Another theme in these songs is the awareness of time. As you grow out of childhood, you begin realizing the passage of time is irreversible, and that's a part of growing into adulthood. We often notice that adolescents seem to have a feeling of invulnerability and immortality. Choices don't really matter; I can always start over again. But we usually outgrow that adolescent attitude in our early 20s. Then you realize that the choices you've made are significant and they have consequences, and you can't go back and start over again. You get that sense in some of these songs that time is being registered in a new way. That's a part of ego development. In the course of ego development, time becomes more and more important, and you start measuring time differently. You start relating to a clock differently because you realize you have deadlines and a shrinking amount of time available.

Ultimately, it's about moving toward a midlife crisis when death anxiety typically sets in. It dawns on you that it's not just other people who are going to die; you are going to die as well. Time is passing, and you can't recapture it. There is no returning to your childhood. There is no going back in time except in memory and fantasy. Time becomes more and more real as the ego passes through these stages of development.

Track 10: *Louder than Bombs*
Louder than Bombs is a statement of empathy. BTS is looking outside their own suffering and toward that of the wider world. They're seeing the suffering of migrants, the suffering of people who are the victims of climate change, or warfare, etc. There

is so much suffering in the world, and it seeps into us and we feel it. BTS is showing their empathy to the suffering of others in the world, including their ARMY of fans. "We feel with you; we know some of you are in really hard places." They are reaching out in solidarity with the suffering of the outside world. They're saying: BTS cares! We feel your pain! This is a sign of maturity.

Track 11: ON

Jung once said, "Send me a sane man, and I will cure him." Sanity is a highly valued virtue and quality. We want to be sane, we want our family members to be sane, we want our society to be sane, but sanity by itself isn't enough. It lacks imagination; it lacks depth. It's basically just common sense, and while we need it and it's valuable, it doesn't nearly satisfy the needs of the psyche for creativity and imagination. A "sane person" is someone who is not in touch with the unconscious. That's what Jung meant: I will take that sane person and put them in contact with the unconscious. That will give them depth. Wholeness can't just be based on rational consciousness.

Jung's basic prescription for wholeness was to contact the unconscious through working with your dreams, active imagination and other techniques, so that you can be in touch with other parts of yourself that we would call, not necessarily insane, but irrational and off the beaten track. That's where your creativity will be; that's where your life energy will come from.

"ON" is also very much about resilience, about overcoming difficulties and suffering and going on. BTS shows a quality that is described in the theory of "antifragility." Antifragility is a quality that things have that allows them to survive severe shocks and traumas. If an object is antifragile, it can fall on a hard surface from a height and not break. Fragile things like glasses and vases break. Your cell phone has been made to be antifragile. You can drop it, it can fall in the toilet, it can fall on the ground, and it usually doesn't break or become nonfunctional. It's antifragile. That's what we strive for when we work with people in psychotherapy, to make them antifragile. We're all going to take hits, blows, setbacks, discouraging times, failures, etc. It's inevitable, and if you're fragile, it will break you. So, to make somebody antifragile is to make them resilient so they can bounce back. They can fall, be hurt emotionally and suffer the pain, and yet they get up and go on. That's what this song is about. Keep on moving, keep on going no matter how bad the times get.

Track 12: *Ugh!*

The song *Ugh!* expresses disgust at people who hide behind masks and direct their anger against others anonymously. It urges a stand against a world dominated by rage. And it gives a glimpse into the pain BTS must have felt as targets of such disguised anger. Trolls and bullies fill all corners of the Internet and social media. You might get a smile when a person sees you, but then that person bullies you on Facebook anonymously. Posts on Twitter and other platforms routinely draw large numbers of bullying "trolls" if the post is at all controversial. A lot of that anger comes out of envy, jealousy, and projection. BTS must get a lot of that. The envy must be enormous from the other K-pop groups and other people who've not been as successful as they have. I'm sure they take a lot of hits. It can really take its toll.

Track 13: *Zero O'Clock*

Zero O'Clock is the midnight hour. It's when the old day ends and a new one begins. It's a song about endings and new beginnings. It's a rebirth song. It's related to Track 9, *My Time*, with the theme of recognition that time marches on. As one leaves childhood and enters adulthood, time takes on new meaning. And one also realizes that there are cycles in time: All things end, and all endings are followed by rebirth into something new. At zero o'clock, aka midnight, one is at the turning point of that transition.

Track 14: *Inner Child*

Inner Child, is sung by V. It's his solo song, and it's fitting that this song is performed by a single voice. It is an intimate account of memories of childhood. This is a song of nostalgia, a tender remembering of experiences from days gone by and wrapped in the warm blankets of maternal nurturance and protection.

The "inner child" is also often related in psychological writings to experiences of trauma in childhood. This phrase became extensively used in studies of early trauma. Donald Kalsched is one of the most significant Jungians to take up the theme of trauma and how children defend themselves against it. It has a trauma and then elaborates a defense system that can be both protective and destructive. Kalsched has a wonderful appreciation for the spirit that the child is protecting, its divine essence. The protective shield that develops is a double-edged sword, because on the one hand it does keep the trauma out in a way, but it also keeps the child separated from life and later the adult separated from life as well.

The *inner child* is also symbolic. The references include memories of childhood, but they also extend out much further in meaning for the present and future. The inner child is not only the child of the past but also the child in the present and the potential for the future. It's an archetype. It's the part of you that's new, has a futuristic orientation, can grow, can develop. The inner child can be very sensitive, as children often are, but it also has tremendous potential. So, when we speak of the inner child, we're speaking of one's potential as well as one's memory.

Track 15: *Friends*

Friends is a duet between Jimin and V. Throughout the lyrics they sing, "Stay here, stay by my side." They've been friends since their school days, and they remain dear to one another. The song is also anticipating an inevitable, at least partial, separation. *Map of the Soul 7* is as a whole about the completion of an opus. The album is announcing this completion and therefore implying also an ending. This is implicit, but it is very noticeable in many of the song. This is the ending of a period or a phase. In the face of this realization, Jimin and V affirm their long friendship, which is precious to them. True friendship between men is something very rare in our world. When friendships are formed at an early age, they have the potential to last for a lifetime. But people's lives take unexpected twists and turns, and friends go in different directions. People grow and change, like snakes who shed their skins, and this may mean they move apart from another. This is something to grieve because it's a loss. *Friends* is a very poignant song.

Track 16: *Moon*

Moon is sung by Jin. It's his solo song. He takes the role of the Moon singing to the Earth, which is the ARMY of BTS fans around the world. It's significant that BTS uses the moon to symbolize the light shining out to the fans. The moon is a light in the darkness. It's very dramatic visually, very romantic. The moon, unlike the sun, is changeable. It goes through phases. Sometimes it's bright, sometimes it's very dim. The song suggests cycles when BTS is sometimes shining brightly and at other times dimly. It's a kind of love song.

Track 17: *Respect*

In a later chapter in this book, titled "The Shadow and the Problem of Violence," I speak to this issue of respect. One of the most frequently cited reasons people give for committing violent acts like murder is that they felt "dissed," that is, *disrespected* in some way. Disrespect feels like humiliation and can be extraordinarily triggering of violent outbursts and lead to catastrophic acts. Disrespect enrages many people. A sensitivity to respect and disrespect is a very important feature in domestic violence. When children don't respect their parents, or parents don't respect their children, or spouses don't respect each other, violent arguments that can lead to violent acts erupt.

BTS sings of respect in this song as the highest and most difficult quality to achieve. In the song they say, it's easy *to say* you respect another person, but to follow through and behave accordingly is another matter. Acting with respect is the critical test. They sing, "*Re-spect* means as it sounds, to literally look again and again, Look again and again and you'll see faults, But you still want to keep looking, despite of that." They're urging us to keep looking at the "other." When you keep looking at someone, you're bound to see their flaws, but the fact that you nonetheless want to keep looking and, I would add, looking without judgment, shows that respect.

Track 18: *We are Bulletproof: The Eternal*
In *We are Bulletproof: The Eternal*, BTS sings altogether: "We were only 7, but we have you all now. We're not afraid anymore, together we are bulletproof." It's an affirmation that they and ARMY are one and together they are invulnerable to the slings and arrows of hate and criticism. They're

bulletproof, they won't go down. To say that they are *eternal* is a very strong statement. It's saying they have overcome time itself. Temporality does not affect them, and many years from now, even after they are dead and gone, they will still be present, and their music will still be inspiring young people. They are putting BTS up there among the stars that never change. It's a very strong claim, and it's also affirming the strength of their unity as a group and of their unity with ARMY fans.

Track 19: *Outro: Ego*
This song is reviewed more thoroughly in Book 3 in the series, *Map of the Soul: Ego*.

Jung once wrote about stepping out of a cloud and suddenly realizing: "I am." It's a numinous moment of revelation, that experience of self-reflection on the part of the ego. I think BTS is closing their album with this affirmation: Yes, we have arrived at this stage of consciousness. The album starts with *Persona*, then moves through *Shadow*, and ends with *Ego*. This is not without meaning. This is a carefully structured, well-built album. The songs open at the surface of the psyche and then moved inward. They experience the shadow, and they end up with a strong ego. This is an important psychological development. The ego gets strengthened by dealing with and integrating the shadow.

BTS arrived at the end of this phase of their development after 7 years of existence together. Hope and maturity accompany them. We'll see what the future holds in store.

Chapter 3
A Review of the
Map of the Soul
By Steven Buser and Leonard Cruz

The Map

This map of the soul has two center points, the *ego* and the *archetypal Self*. The *archetypal Self* lies at the core of our *ego*. Because this idea is difficult to depict, we have represented it as a cone through which the *ego* funnels into the *archetypal* Self. We will talk more of these structures shortly.

In the upper righthand corner of the map appears a large eye that looks out toward a village or, more accurately, gazes out to the entire world, taking in the totality of what we physically see, hear, smell, and touch. *Ego* perceives reality through the senses. The eye sits atop a range of mountains representing the *persona*. The *persona* is located between the *ego* and the surrounding world since it mediates our presentation to the outside world. Most of the world does

Persona

Animus Anima

External World

Ego

Shadow

Archetypal Self

Persona

C
A

C
A

C
A

Complex

C
A

C
A
Archetypal Core of Complex

Primordial Fire
(deep within collective Unconscious)

Illustration by Steven Buser

not see what lies beyond the *persona*, just as a tall mountain range blocks our view of what is beyond. *Persona* is the *mask* we show those around us.

To the far left side of the mountains lies the *shadow* with the *ego* lying midway between. *Shadow* is depicted as a hooded figure. It is no accident that it is found directly opposite to the *persona* on the other side of the mountain range (from the perspective of the *ego*). The *shadow* is the opposite of the *persona*. Whatever positive, acceptable face we show the world through our *persona* is balanced by a darker, unacknowledged, and opposite figure that forms our *shadow*. The *shadow* carries all the unwanted, shameful, unacceptable parts of our psyche. We bury them deep within, hoping they won't be discovered. The *shadow* exists in the unconscious.

In the upper left side of the map, a region that is still in the unconscious realm lie the *anima* and *animus*. These are opposite-gendered, unconscious figures in our soul. The masculine figure is depicted as a warrior, while the feminine figure is dressed in full-length chiton, a type of tunic. The classical Jungian view is that a man possesses a feminine *anima* connecting him to the deeper levels of his unconscious, while a woman possesses a masculine *animus* connecting her to the depths of her unconscious.

Scattered throughout the unconscious lie numerous ovals with a "C" for *complexes* in the middle and a funnel tapering down to a letter "*A*" for *arche-*

type, which is at the core of a complex. We will explain these later.

Finally, at the bottom of this map are found the flames of the *primordial fire*. This image reminds us that the collective unconscious underlies the entirety of the map. It is here where primitive forces dwell and potent symbols, fears, and inspirations gradually emerge.

The External World

The external world is the easiest part of the map to understand. It represents everything we know as our world. It is everything we can touch, see, and hear and everything present in the physical world with which we interact, including people, objects, and other creatures. The external world contrasts with our internal experience. Our internal experience is harder to grasp and understand, particularly the unconscious realm of which we are not usually aware.

The Ego

The *ego* rests on the surface of the unconscious and occupies the center of consciousness. It is the "I" who speaks, and it is what *I* am aware of when *I* contemplate myself. It lies on the boundary between what we know and what we don't know. It is what we understand consciously of our experience of being human. It acts and sets projects in motion, while encompassing all the traits and characteristics by which we consciously "know ourselves." It is informed and affected by all our memories, traumas, emotions, and facts as well as everything we can consciously sense in our bodies. When we have a "flash of insight," it is often the awareness of something unconscious breaking though to our conscious *ego* awareness.

The Persona

The *persona*, the mountain range, separates our conscious *ego* from the external world and interacts with it. The eye between the *ego* and the external world emphasizes the fact that we look out to the world from our *ego*'s perspective. It is through our senses that we perceive the world around us, and this is represented by the eye looking out. What the world sees as it looks back at us is our *persona*. Thus, in this map, when friends, family, or really anyone looks at us and forms an opinion of us, they are not looking inside our *ego*, but rather at the *persona*, the mask we allow them to see. They see *persona*; they never see the "true us," only the part of ourselves that the *persona* allows them to see. Our *persona* varies, depending on what role we are in. At work, I might be a doctor. Perhaps I dress the part of a doctor by wearing a white coat or other professional clothes. I use language common to physicians, "doctor talk." I sound professional and may even find myself using big words and professional jargon that reinforces my identity and perhaps convinces me and others of my standing. My work *persona* allows me to function more freely and smoothly in my role. When I go home at night, however, if I were to forget to take off my "doctor *persona*" and not put on my "spouse *persona*," bad things will happen. I might order my spouse around, use wordy or professional jargon, insist on things being done my way, etc. At home, the aspects of my *persona* identified with my doctor *persona* are no longer adaptive; it is actually mal-adaptive. At home, I had better put on my "spouse *persona*" or my "father *persona*." With these *personas*, I am less professional; I am more likely to laugh, joke and roll around on the floor with my children. We put on a vast array of *personas* in the course of our lives, including student, friend, mentor, mentee, athlete, partygoer, rock star, social activist, etc.

The *Shadow*

Our *shadow* is the contrary image of our *persona*, its opposite. For every aspect of how we try to present ourselves to the world through our *persona*, an opposite part of our personality gets split off and stored in the *shadow*. If I have worked to make my *persona* come across as a friendly, helpful, and encouraging person, that means that the opposite of those traits, an unfriendly, unhelpful, discouraging person, becomes split off and deposited in my unconscious *shadow*. The intensity of this phenomenon appears to vary in direct proportion with how intense and one-sided my *persona* becomes. A person who presents his or her *persona* to others as an extremely righteous, pious and devoted person lacking any anger or negativity is likely creating an unconscious *shadow* with powerful, cruel, immoral, and irreverent qualities. When the *shadow* makes its presence known, it can be very energetic and forceful in the way it expresses the opposite characteristics. The news has been full of pious preachers speaking out intensely against behaviors they regard as sinful, only to find themselves scandalously caught in those very same actions. One explanation of this is that the more pious their *persona* becomes, the more energized and immoral their *shadow* becomes. Often it is only a matter of time before the unacceptable *shadow* will erupt and become exposed to the public. This sort of *reversal* can be shocking, but it can also be the beginning of a new and more authentic life if handled properly.

Typically, unless we have done a lot of personal work on ourselves, the contents of our *shadow* are hidden and unknown to us. The less we understand about our *shadow* side, the more likely we are to unknowingly act from it, often in ways that hurt others. It is crucial for us to recognize we have a *shadow* side and take steps to deal with it in healthy ways. This consists mostly of becoming conscious of aspects of *shadow* through paying attention to our dreams, to what we find objectionable in others, to what we envy, and by exploring the moments of *reversals* when the *shadow* erupts.

Anima and Animus

Buried within our unconscious lies another figure that holds the neglected sides of our masculinity or femininity. One hundred years ago, as Carl Jung was developing these theories, gender was more rigidly defined within society. It was seldom tolerated in the Victorian Age for men to show much of their feminine side or vice versa. Thus, a man who went through life embodying mostly masculine qualities remained unaware of an undeveloped and unconscious feminine figure in his psyche that Jung called the *anima*. It is through the *anima* that a man is able to connect with his softer, more soulful, and perhaps more creative side. When he tears up, swells with intense emotions, or is more driven by the heart than the head, he is likely connecting to his *anima*. This *anima* might come to him in dreams as a sensual or soulful woman. She is his guide to this deeper place within his personality. She is pregnant with new life, heralding the future.

Traditionally, women had the opposite development challenge to their identity. They were discouraged from pursuing demanding, male-dominated careers and rarely pursued public roles of power and authority. An unconscious masculine figure typically lived hidden away in their unconscious, a personality with strength, determination, and warriorlike power that Jung called the *animus*. In dreams, this figure often comes to women as a powerful male figure.

In the second half of a woman's life, she might distance herself from an overly nurturing role and develop a second career with a stronger, more forceful, and public personality. At such times, her *animus* is surfacing.

This paradigm has shifted dramatically over the last few decades as gender became more fluid within individuals and society in general. Men are no longer forced into solely masculine expressions of their personality, just as women are allowed more freedom of expression. Nonetheless, whatever gender elements we incline toward, the opposite gender develops unconscious power within our *anima/animus*. Connecting to those opposite gender traits allows us to become more whole and complete.

Complexes

Scattered throughout the unconscious zone of our map are numerous *complexes*. We have symbolized them as a "C" within an oval that funnels down toward the letter "*A*." Each one of us has countless *complexes* within our unconscious.

A *complex* is a sort of subpersonality with its own set of charged emotions that cluster around certain areas or triggers in our lives, often a trauma. You have probably already heard many of the common complexes that have made their way into our vocabulary such as *mother complex, father complex, money complex, Oedipal complex, hero complex, Napoleon complex, Peter Pan complex, lover complex,* etc. Just hearing the title of the complexes likely brings to mind a fair amount of what they encompass. Thus, a person gripped by a money complex may irrationally fear poverty and financial need. Even though he has plenty of money, his fear drives him to hoard more and more. One might name it a *Scrooge complex* after the Charles Dickens character in *A Christmas Carol*. Those who struggle with a *hero complex*, on the other hand, may find themselves irrationally drawn toward rescuing others who may not even need their help. The more powerful a *complex*, the less aware we will be when we fall into it and the more our behavior is controlled by it. Our friends, family, and lovers, though, are painfully aware when we are in the grips of these *complexes*, even as we irrationally defend our behaviors.

A particular point of Jungian psychology is that at the core of every complex lies an *archetype*, in our drawings noted as the letter "*A.*" Thus, at the heart of someone's *hero complex* lies the *archetype* of the hero. This archetype is present in hero images known throughout history and embodies all the heroic traits to which humanity has ever been exposed. We can imagine the world's most powerful hero, Hercules for example, lying at the heart of this *complex*. It is that intense energy that a person in the grips of a hero complex is tapping into. These moments can be precarious for those trapped in the complex or, on the other hand, may even result in admirable deeds.

The Archetypal Self

Within the framework of Jungian psychology, the *ego* is technically a complex where we hold our conscious self-identity. Remembering that at the core of every *complex* lies an *archetype*, within the core of the *ego complex* lies the *archetypal Self*. It can be referred to by its full name, the *archetypal Self*, or simply the *Self*. By convention we capitalize the *Self* to note its elements of totality and even sacredness, similar to how *God* & *He/His/Him* are capitalized in the Christian scripture. The *Self* is humanity's (as well as each individual's) grand organizing principle. While many have referred to the *archetypal Self* as God, it may be better to think of it as godlike with infinite, boundless possibilities that we often associate with phrases like a *higher power* or a sum of all the conscious and unconscious elements within our universe. It is *the Alpha and the Omega,* the beginning and the end, the *totality* and the *singularity* combined as one. It is hard to write about the *archetypal Self* without lapsing into mysticism and using grandiose metaphors. It is truly ineffable, and words fail to capture it.

The Primordial Fire

We added the *primordial fire* to the bottom of our map in an effort to show some of the profound archetypal forces underlying these structures. The *primordial fire* represents the initial source of psychic energy and the animating forces throughout human history and even the history of the universe. It drives survival, evolution, creativity, and such instincts as sexuality and hunger. When we are depressed, we have lost contact with the *primordial fire*. When we are manic, we may become engulfed in its flames. At times, the fire envelopes the planet, such as during the world wars or at other times of profound conflict or social upheaval. It has deep veins in the psyche, and it runs like lava beneath the crust of the earth, erupting during these intense times.

This is a collective fire that has been burning throughout the ages. Billy Joel's haunting words, "We didn't start the fire, It was always burning since the world's been turning," powerfully capture the metaphor of its ceaseless flames.

Before you dive more deeply into the ideas of *shadow*, here are a few suggestions that emerge from this map.

A Few Precepts to Keep in Mind....

Don't let the world define you. Blaze your own path through!

This is particularly hard for young people. There is so much to do in those early years—excel in high school and college, find the right career, find a life partner, raise children, etc. There is nothing wrong with these things, and indeed many of them are important to pursue, but sometimes these expectations are thrust upon us against our will, and they run contrary to our true nature. Looking through the lens of our map, we must be careful that the *persona* we construct retains authenticity; we must listen to our *shadow's* ferocity; we must avoid being ensnared by our *complexes* and we must tap into the inspiration of our *anima/animus*. Only by encompassing this totality, both conscious and unconscious, can we hope to discern our unique path and follow our true self.

Listen to your nighttime dreams. Keep a dream journal.

A key principle of Jungian psychology is the crucial importance of our dreams during sleep. Dreams bubble up from the collective unconscious and are informed by the *archetypal Self*. All dreams have meaning for us, telling us something we do not yet know but need to know. Write down your nighttime dreams in a journal. Reflect on them the next day and ask yourself what the various elements of the dream remind you of. Avoid the simplicity of a "dream symbol dictionary," as you will need to do the hard work yourself and not rely on someone else's interpretations. If you can, work with a Jungian analyst or other therapist who works with dreams from that perspective. Join or start a dream group where people share and reflect on dreams in a nonjudgmental and noncritical environment. Use your dreams to develop your own personalized *Map of the Soul*.

Listen to your daytime dreams. Keep a daytime journal.

Consider keeping a daytime journal as well for any thoughts, emotions, creative impulses, or inspirations you might have. You can even write out dialogues with other parts of yourself, including *shadow* figures, *anima* figures or characters from your nighttime dreams. Notice the occasions when you undergo a reversal, and the *shadow* erupts. Ask questions and get to know these interior parts of yourself. Wonder about the present and dream about the future. Remain curious about all elements of yourself, both your interior world as well as how you interact with others. This curiosity will keep you on your path of growth.

Stay aware of your dark side (your *shadow*). Own it when it flares up and utilize its strength.

Unfortunately, ignoring our dark side is a common trap that we all fall into from time to time. We convince ourselves that we have tamed our inner darkness, only to have it reappear abruptly. When our darkness erupts, it has free rein to plunge us into various destructive paths. It is vitally important that we stay aware of our *shadow* and the hurtful prejudices, stereotypes, and superior attitudes we hold.

Stay connected to your *shadow*. Dialogue with it, listen to it, and observe how it is projected onto people and situations in your life, like a movie projected onto a screen. Acknowledge to others when your darker self has taken over and you have done things that you regret. Growth and individuation can only happen if we stay aware of our dark self and are willing to confront our less appealing qualities.

Stay connected to your body.

Avoid the trap of remaining too much in your head and disconnected from your body and the outside world. This is a trap that many Jungians and other intellectual types fall into. Looking solely at ideas, concepts, and archetypes without also looking at how they embody themselves in our physical world can prove to be a costly mistake. Listen to your body. Try to understand when it hurts, grumbles, or has a painful memory buried within it. Enjoy your body when it wants to dance, run, or play with reckless abandon.

Stay creative no matter what, and express this creativity.

Stay connected to whatever forms of creativity enliven your soul. Expressions are not only works of art like paint on a canvas, but include dance, prose, molding clay, playing music, using your voice, and countless other expressions. Creativity is a great way of tapping into the *primordial energy* in a healthy way that fuels our growth and individuation.

Know something about your personality make up, its strengths and challenges.

Stay curious about who you are and how your personality challenges and strengthens you. Seek an understanding of Carl Jung's ideas of introversion, extroversion, thinking, feeling, intuition, etc. Knowing who we are in these ways and how we engage with important people in our lives not only helps us to understand our behaviors but also helps us optimize how we engage with others.

Remember the arc of life and that young adulthood, midlife and elder years have very different callings.

It is important to consider where we are in our life's course. In our early years, we are typically building our psychic structures, our personality, our desires, our relationships, and our vocations. Hopefully, we do so with passion and a sense of calling. By midlife, we have already built these structures and we may be more occupied with a productive career, a growing family, or other challenges.

Often in midlife, there is a need for a significant course correction. We must stay alert and listen for that. By our elder years, we are on the other side of the arc of life, declining in some areas while deepening in others. We are typically exiting careers and mentoring those around us. We are often more spiritual and are nurturing our inner connection to a higher reality. While each of us needs to find our own expressions within these typical patterns, it is helpful to remember that the map serves us differently depending on the stage of our life's journey.

Remain true to yourself.

We must remain true to ourselves! But what does that really mean? Of course, it means different things to different people. We propose that it involves the vital quest of discovering what you are uniquely called to in this world. It is breaking free of the molds that others attempt to put you in as you claim your unique inheritance as a member of the human race. Regardless of how your true path unfolds, you must at all costs, listen to your gentle, whispering inner voice and honor the signs that life offers you.

Chapter 4
Murray Stein on *Shadow*
Interviewed by Leonard Cruz

Explorations of Shadow

Len Cruz: Would you please explain what the *shadow* is?

Murray Stein: Jung came up with this term, *shadow*—it's something of an original image intended to refer to the parts of the personality of which we are not aware, that are in a way behind our backs. The *shadow* exists on the fringe of our awareness and is difficult to see directly. You might also think of the *shadow* as the sum of our motivations, thoughts, feelings, and behaviors that we would not be proud of or for which we don't want to accept responsibility. It is the dark part of our personality of which we are ashamed or that we cannot acknowledge. Things about our personality that we are ashamed of or that might be difficult to acknowledge are relegated to the *shadow*.

Len Cruz: How much of what comprises the *shadow* is dependent on things that are objectively distasteful or objectionable, and how much is colored by our subjective impression of what would be objectionable?

Murray Stein: I think the *shadow* is mostly shaped by our subjective sense of the world around us. For example, our feelings of self-esteem are highly dependent on what other people think of us. So, if we're in a culture or a family where certain qualities are not appreciated or valued, we would try to stay away from those qualities though they're a part of ourselves. For instance, some people are naturally very outgoing, or in Jungian terms we say extroverted. Now, if they are in a culture that does not look kindly upon people who are outgoing, too friendly or too demonstrative in public, such a person will try to tone down those qualities in their personality. One tries to shut off or put away those motivations and behaviors. So, this helps us understand how something that might be a natural part of ourselves can be discouraged or associated with feelings of shame or social disapproval. We recognize that this process is a subjective response to our world.

Of course, the surrounding culture exerts objective effects based on what is culturally unacceptable, and a person adapts to this subjectively. The *shadow* is largely a product of our conformity or adaptation to the culture around us. The culture's judgment is somewhat objective, and our judgements about what our surrounding culture values is primarily subjective.

Len Cruz: Conformity to the culture around us seems to be a necessity.

Murray Stein: It's natural to conform to the social world around us because it's natural for us to want to be respected and esteemed. Suppose you grow up in a criminal family where criminal behavior is valued in your family but not in the wider culture. Within the family context, your criminal behavior would be a source of respect and esteem, but you wouldn't want to show that in the general culture, or you would be punished or imprisoned.

Len Cruz: Staying with that idea for just a moment, would the *shadow* of a person raised in that sort of environment reflect features that we normally might think of as noble and socially acceptable?

Murray Stein: Exactly! Actions that might be disapproved of in the greater society might be highly esteemed within a smaller society. In a criminal family, things that are normally shunned in society might be required, respected, and produce great benefits. The makeup of the *shadow* really depends upon what you're conforming to.

Len Cruz: C.G. Jung stated, "We need more understanding of human nature, because the only real danger is man himself." What insights can you offer about the implications of this quote for the individual and for the collective work humanity is called to do?

Murray Stein: I think what Jung was referring to there was a tendency we have to enact our impulses and justify them. In other words, if a country would feel itself in danger from another country, it could "defend itself" by launching a preemptive strike on the other country. Though the aggressor country might feel justified and within that national culture the first strike might appear defensible, looked at from another perspective, it would appear quite different. It could bring catastrophic results and even unleash a nuclear war. This is what Jung feared. The point is that it's easy for us to justify, explain, or defend our impulsive behaviors within a certain set of conventional and self-serving expectations. But in a larger sense, we can see that these sorts of actions and reactions are very dangerous and destructive.

This type of behavior happens all the time on an interpersonal level. We enact impulses, and if somebody questions us about them, we defend them vigorously, because we are confident in our rationale for them. However, if we put ourselves in the other person's shoes and look at ourselves from their perspective, we may be able to see that we are overreacting or using the situation as an occasion for violence or aggression or opportunism. The primary goal of becoming conscious of *shadow* is to step outside of one's self a bit, and look at one's self from another perspective.

Remember, we can't generally see our own *shadow*, although we are enacting it continually in our lives. Occasionally, can we step outside our self-justified perspective to see what we are really doing unconsciously? Think of the *shadow* as a double agent. In one respect, we appear to ourselves as conscious, light, bright, perfectly justified. And yet there's another character in us that possesses hidden motives and agendas, and these are enacted at the same time. This is our *shadow*. We are both. Both are housed in the same body.

Len Cruz: Can we say that it is visible to others, but to a large extent, if not almost entirely, it's disguised to ourselves?

Murray Stein: Yes. We can't see it ourselves, but others can see it. If you're standing in bright sunlight and facing toward the sun, you can't see that you even have a *shadow*, let alone what it looks like. There's nothing shadowy in front of you. But if you turn around and look the other way, or if somebody takes a picture of you from a third position, the *shadow* behind you will be revealed. It's usually embarrassing.

Len Cruz: When you speak of stepping outside of yourself, or you say there are occasions when you might get a glimpse of that, what sort of occasions or events do you refer to?

Murray Stein: This sometimes happens in therapy. A person describes an event that took place recently. Say they've gotten into a dispute with their husband or their wife. As they're describing it, and the therapist is quietly listening, they might start seeing themselves through the eyes of the therapist, a witness. Harold Bloom described this as overhearing yourself. You hear or see yourself from another person's position. The therapist may be saying nothing or may ask a question, and suddenly a person will start reflecting, "Oh, yes. Maybe there was another agenda afoot. Maybe I was unnecessarily defensive or aggressive." This can be a shocking realization. Even shattering.

Len Cruz: Why is it that the discourse we have aloud—say in the company of a therapist who is quietly listening—can evoke a new perspective in ways the chatter in our head fails to achieve?

Murray Stein: Well, the discourse in one's own head is trapped in subjectivity. The discourse that is said to another person echoes back, and so the other person becomes like a mirror. You can see things in a mirror that you can't see when you're just looking straight out of your eyes. To begin with, you start seeing yourself. That's why therapy can be so effective; a person is allowed just to speak, and the therapist is quietly mirroring. They start hearing themselves in another way. This can also happen when someone films you and you later watch yourself. I had this experience years ago. I was on a program, and the discussion was being filmed. I watched the film afterward, I saw myself on the film in a way I had never experienced myself. I asked my wife about this, and she confirmed what I saw. It was an eye-opener.

Len Cruz: Did you see things you found objectionable, that you wouldn't have otherwise been able to have observed?

Murray Stein: Not grossly objectionable, but things that other people had said about me and I had brushed off. At most, I had wondered why are these things were being said about me. A lot of people don't like to see themselves on film; they don't like to see what film reveals. Why is that? It's because watching the film, you see yourself in a more objective way. You may have an image of yourself, of the kind of person you are, what your qualities are like, and how you come across to others. Seeing yourself on film can disrupt that. Let's say it's a difference between subjective self-perception and objective self-perception. On the film, you see yourself as an object, not as the subject. When you see yourself as an object, you see flaws and other features you ordinarily are blind to or deny. It's not unlike when you look in the mirror and you see flaws on your skin and wrinkles and you think, "Oh my goodness. I'm going to have to do something about that. I need to clean myself up." That's what therapy is really about; it is coming to a place where you can see yourself more objectively and start making some changes based on your new consciousness.

Len Cruz: Perhaps then, we should distrust our subjective self-impressions and pursue opportunities that have the potential to hold up a mirror for us to look at, that is a more objective perspective.

Murray Stein: Yes, except it's not usually pleasant when you see yourself objectively like that. Most people don't look for opportunities to do that. When such opportunities do appear, they tend to look the other way, to avoid what they might encounter. If they have some courage and they really want to become more self-aware, they'll look at themselves, and they'll watch themselves, and they will become more conscious. The best actors must do this. They have to be straight with themselves or they will get stuck in lazy habits.

Len Cruz: What other examples, beyond therapy, can you point to where one might encounter and become conscious of aspects of the *shadow*?

Murray Stein: We know that what is unconscious to a person is projected onto external objects or people. What that means is that a person experiences those unconscious qualities, those features of their own personality, not as part of themselves but as qualities in somebody else. It is often difficult to sort out the difference between perception and pro-jection. What are you perceiving in another person, let's say in your friend, your partner, your business associate, your boss, or your student that is really a part of them, and what are you adding to that, or layering over it that rightfully belongs to you but that you've disowned or disavowed? It's worth asking the question even if you can't answer it definitively.

One way to catch a glimpse of your *shadow* is to examine the people you really dislike. Look at the disagreeable qualities that you see in them and then ask yourself, "Where are those qualities in me?" Say you're a quite successful and hardworking sort of person who has earned your way to your present status by dint of your own efforts, and you really dislike people who are passive, lazy, and always looking for a handout. You may find that you have a very strong emotional reaction to those people and very little empathy for them. "Why aren't they more like me?" you ask. "I had to work hard for what I have, etc." We all know such stories in our own families and in the society at large. To catch hold of the *shadow*, you might ask yourself, "Where am I like that? When do I think like that?" Or perhaps, "Do I envy them?" This can put you in touch with the *shadow*, because the *shadow* is something that is very different from you. It is your unlived life. When we project the *shadow*, we put ourselves above and look down on the "other." We don't feel connected. We tend to judge. This is a reflection of how we judge ourselves. We condemn our laziness and don't let ourselves take a decent vacation while condemning those who are always seemingly on vacation.

Len Cruz: Would we be pushing this approach too far to suppose that a person envies these qualities they find in the other?

Murray Stein: Not consciously, but there is the fact of unconscious envy. Envy is a part of almost everybody's *shadow*. Most people loudly deny that they're envious, because that is really a quality that very few people want to or can admit to.

Len Cruz: Earlier you explained that the *shadow* enacts our impulses, and you seem to be adding that a road to discovering our *shadow* often involves investigating the domains in which we feel strong passion or pathos.

Murray Stein: In the vicinity of the *shadow* you have strong feelings, and they are not positive feelings. People can become very passionate indeed in their reactions against *shadow* figures. There are certain figures in history, for example, or certain people in our contemporary culture that it's easy to project our *shadows* on, because they have qualities, objectively, that are suitable hooks, as we say, to catch the projection of *shadow*.

For example, political leaders will often catch the projection of the darkest *shadow*. We tend to see them splitting the world between good and evil. Presently in the U.S.A., President Donald Trump catches a lot of projections. This doesn't mean that he doesn't possess these qualities that are also projected on him. Bear in mind that one can oppose the things that he's doing, but when people get very passionate about that, and overly exaggerate the objectionable qualities, they fail to take into account a more complete and complex picture. Someone like the current president represents the collective *shadow* of a nation that is itself trying to hide the very qualities he reveals so openly and strikingly. The more complex picture is that the nation has a *shadow*. This president reveals it. When we feel revulsion for him, we are facing the nation's *shadow*. And this is shocking. But other countries could tell us a lot about the *shadow* of America in the world, and it would be consistent with what we see in this president.

Let's consider racism. President Trump is often branded as a racist, which he may well be. I haven't studied that carefully. But America is notorious for hiding its heritage and continuing evidence of racism. When a figure appears who catches that projection, they are the recipient of a collective *shadow* projection. Many people participate in this social phenomenon but are unwilling to admit it. So, if I'm an unconscious racist, I'd love to find somebody out there who's an explicit racist, so I can label them and attack them, or criticize them. This makes it easier for me to avoid a genuine confrontation of my own racism. Projections onto a very visible figure as being racist permits me to remain unconscious to my own racism. I feel pure and project all the bad onto him. This is classic *shadow* projection. The object carrying the projection is a scapegoat.

Len Cruz: The person who is certain they are not a racist and struggles with America's legacy of racist practices might have just as hard a time as the overt racist in seeing *shadow's* influence, right?

Murray Stein: Yes. I don't believe there's any-body who's not racist to some degree. If you think that you're not racist at all, I think you're quite unconscious. You might not be a racist in the strong sense of the word that you want to commit violence, but you have racist reactions. Everybody does. The person who can face their *shadow* and say, "Yes, I have racist reactions, too," has a much better chance of counteracting their racism than the person who denies it. The person who denies it, enacts it unconsciously. The person who admits it and takes it into account may try to offset it consciously, or at least try to not let it interfere with their conscious activities and decisions.

Len Cruz: It would be naïve to think that in the political arena both sides aren't simultaneously casting their projections on the other. In a sense, intolerance of the other's opinions and perspective is another clue that we are in the vicinity of the *shadow*, right?

Murray Stein: Yes, we are intolerant of *shadow*; that's why it's *shadow*. We don't want it. We don't like it. And it's very difficult to have a conversation with a *shadow* bearer. We feel revulsion. We want to get away from them.

I think that at bottom of the *shadow* is evil per se or what Jung refers to as absolute evil. In a chapter in his book *Aion*, where he's talking about *shadow*, he implies that it is fairly easy to become aware of one's personal *shadow*, which is probably an exaggeration, but he goes on to say that it is a rare person who can look into the face of absolute evil. It's so horrible.

What is absolute evil? It is cold. It is brutal. It is an *ego* that is absolutely self-centered. It is at the core of the selfish, egotistical personality that we all have. It is that "I" in us that wants what it wants, when it wants it, at any cost, and will go to any length to get it. That is the essence of the *shadow* part of the personality. We don't want to see that part of ourselves. It shocks us. We don't want to admit it to ourselves, let alone to others. We shiver when we see somebody who exemplifies it, as happens in the movies sometimes. The figure who embodies absolute evil is both fascinating and frightening to us.

Len Cruz: Murray, let me ask you. Anyone who's has raised young children has seen examples of willful, self-centered toddlers who act like little tyrants; some people refer to this phase as the terrible twos. At this stage there is often very little awareness of the impact this behavior and this self-centered attitude has on others. If that is continued into adulthood, this might become pure evil of the sort you are describing.

Murray Stein: Yes, and in later years it simply goes hidden. It is still there. Somewhere within each of us is a terrible 2-year-old. There is an inner child within each of us, but it is hidden from us, and we do not want to admit it. We usually manage not to enact it totally, but it's always there, and it's always at work.

Len Cruz: What role does conscience play? Is it a tempering influence?

Murray Stein: Conscience is a complicated topic. On the one hand, it's our introjected values from culture and from our parents. It speaks to things like keeping ourselves clean, being nice to other people, and respecting other people's property. The 10 Commandments and religious codes contribute contents to this level of conscience. We learn all these things, and we take them in, and they become a part of what we also call the watchful "superego." Our conscience functions like an inner judge that prevents us from exercising impulses that would violate those rules. That's a part of conscience. It's simply the rules of the family or the culture taken in and made a part of ourselves as an inner watchdog.

But that's a rather superficial level of conscience. It's something the children learn at quite an early age. Their good conduct is based on the fear of being punished for breaking the rules; out of fear they become good boys and girls and conform to the conventions of the society they grow up in. However, there is a deeper kind of conscience, which is what we can call an innate sense of justice and fairness. It's like we have a good angel on one shoulder and a bad angel on the other. The bad angel is the one that wants us to be 2 years old and enact our egotism and selfishness. The good angel has a sense of justice, and this one puts us on an equal footing with everybody else. It says, "Would you want other people to do that to you?" It is the root of "do unto others as you would have them do unto you," or "do to others what you would like them to do for you." From these two voices you start getting a sense of balancing your *ego* interests with other people's interests. Sometimes one weighs more (self-interest), sometimes the other weighs more (altruism). There is a pendulum effect. In a sense, one is the *shadow* of the other.

We are constructed of opposites. If you listen to the good angel all the time, the bad angel doesn't go away. It's there, but it works in a very underhanded way, behind your back. Your selfish agendas are there, only they are well hidden. Jung said about his pastor father that in public he was all good but at home he had a very bad temper. You may be more likely to witness the *shadow* when a good person becomes exhausted, stressed, or tired; they let their guard down, and a different personality appears. We saw this recently in Pope Francis, when he slapped the hand of a woman in the audience who had tried to hold onto his sleeve. He was tired and reacted with strong anger and aggression. Later he apologized, of course.

What we have within is a kind of Dr. Jekyll and Mr. Hyde phenomenon. Mr. Hyde's a nice man, but Dr. Jekyll is a *shadow* character who works his evil at night. Our goal as Jungians is to work toward wholeness, which means nurturing a balance between self-interest and the interests of others. Generally, we work toward balancing the opposites, not choosing one over the other.

Len Cruz: There appear to be two extremes in this regard. At one end is a person whose self-absorption is so thorough that they're incapable of recognizing the other. At the other extreme is the person who has such a well-developed conscience and moral compass that they can't avoid thinking of the other.

Murray Stein: That's a possible construct. There are people with no conscience whom we call psychopaths or sociopaths, and a lot of them are locked up and imprisoned if caught. These people are cold-blooded; they have no conscience. They don't care about anything other than themselves. But, on the other end of the spectrum, we know there are people who are so other-focused as to be almost incapable of pursuing their own interests, and this is its own sort of problem. They don't look out for themselves enough and are too self-sacrificing. In some cases, they become busybodies, and they want to help other people even when other people don't want their help. They tend to neglect themselves. What these people are not accepting in themselves is their own natural egotism and self-interest. They're repressing that, so this natural egotism becomes *shadow*. Jung said, at one point, "It's unhealthy to be too good." In therapy we have to help them become more self-assertive and stand up for themselves. Because the natural egotism becomes *shadow*, and when they do enact egotistical or selfish impulses, they are prone to be excessive. They're guilty about things they had nothing to do with.

Now, there might be exceptions whom we would call saints, people who are perhaps built in slightly different ways. I haven't had the opportunity to interview any of those people.

Len Cruz: As a person recovers aspects that were part of the *shadow*, do we see a tempering of those aspects in the *persona* that may had been over exaggerated? Is it a sort of corollary with the *personas*?

Murray Stein: Yes. As you move away from one-sidedness toward balancing the opposites, let's say between *persona* and *shadow*, eventually both sides change. So, the *persona* would adjust itself and take up some of the *shadow* components. Let's say aggression, for instance, is in the *shadow*. When integrated, the person would become more self-assertive as a consequence, and the *persona* would change accordingly. This is an important aspect of psychological development. The *shadow* side would be less unconscious and less prone to be projected onto others. When the opposites aren't pushed apart so far, they become complements, and they supplement each other. Along with that, one doesn't have to be so ashamed of the *shadow* part of one's self. One can be more open about it. The *shadow* is part of the whole and recognized as such.

When you see somebody who's really done this work, they're relaxed. They're not trying too hard to be good. If you point out certain features that in a public setting might be seen as not perfect or not the best, they accept it gracefully. They aren't proud of it, but they don't try to deny it defensively. They can apologize, as we saw Pope Francis do so well.

Len Cruz: It's been said that if you really want to know yourself, just ask the people around you; ask your spouse or your friends. Can you comment a little about how that's also an avenue of discovery?

Murray Stein: What this means is that you are asking for a picture of yourself from another person's perspective. The problem with this approach is that the person you ask might have an agenda of their own and be trying to put you in your place, and so they could exaggerate your *shadow* aspects. Nevertheless, over time, if you listen carefully to the people around you—your coworkers, your fellow citizens, your neighbors, your friends, your family members—you will get a picture of yourself, a portrait that would include your *shadow* aspects. If they love you, they will say things like, "Well, I really like this about you, but when you do that, I don't like it."

Len Cruz: We should probably listen for recurring themes, in particular the ones we would tend to push away, discount, or defend against, right?

Murray Stein: Yes, list especially to what you become defensive about, or just don't recognize, because this is unconscious to you. Let me say that one other place where you can discover things about your *shadow* is in your dreams. We talked about projections. We talked about getting feedback from other people. If you look at your dreams over a period of time, you'll see certain characters appearing and reappearing who are not the "I" in the dream. They are generally characters of the same sex or gender that you are, but they are considerably different in ways that are not better or noble but are unwanted and undesirable. Maybe they're more aggressive, more hostile, more sexual, and you might have difficulty allowing such characteristics into your everyday life fully.

If you look at those and ask yourself, "Where am I like that? When am I like that? Can I get a feeling for that part of me?" you can gain insight and understanding of your *shadow*. This is to interpret the dreams on a subjective level. In other words, you assume those figures in the dreams are parts of you and not somebody else. This is another way to start getting a sense of your *shadow*.

For instance, I know a man who's had a lot of dreams about unruly young teenagers. At one time he had been a schoolteacher and had difficulty in his classes with some of these adolescents. Over and over again, he had dreams in which he was in a classroom with very unruly teenagers. He is himself a very well-put-together, constructed adult and now an elderly gentleman.

Len Cruz: Not somebody you would describe as unruly.

Murray Stein: Exactly. The adolescents in his dreams are unruly parts of himself that he hasn't managed to take into his conscious personality enough. After a period of time when he had allowed himself to be a little unruly and had gotten into some difficulties with them, he told me a couple of dreams in which the schoolchildren were behaving much better. I think maybe the unruliness was coming more into his conscious personality, and he could accept it and live it in a somewhat conscious way. The unruly teenagers were changing in his dreams. He needs to become more unruly, and the dreams figures will change for the better. That's a sign of integration.

Len Cruz: What other clues might someone look for to determine if figures in a dream are carrying *shadow*?

Murray Stein: I'm thinking now of a man I worked with many years ago in analysis who discovered a method for letting his *shadow*-self speak. It was called the two-hand method. You write something on a piece of paper with your dominant hand, and then you let your nondominant hand answer, back and forth. He was surprised by what the left hand was trying to say to him. This was a piece of himself left behind long ago in his childhood. The left hand was about 6 years old. He was 50 years old. The 6-year-old was expressing himself as being very unhappy. The 50-year-old man asked, "Why are you unhappy? What's the matter?" The left hand, the child, said: "I want to draw and paint, and you don't let me. You don't give me any space and time to do what I want to do." He remembered that when he was about that age, his mother thought he had no talent for art, so she urged him to focus on his academic studies, and so he left the artistic part of himself behind. Now the 50-year-old went out and bought some paints and materials to create art, and the little boy started painting. That reduced the unhappiness of the little boy. His *shadow* integration came about this through the right hand communicating with the left hand.

This is one way to let these unruly parts speak and have a voice, to find out what they want. When you give them a little space to do it, they aren't so unruly anymore and actually become an important part of your creativity.

Len Cruz: When the child figures in our psyche are not tended to, they will often afflict us. Can you speak to that?

Murray Stein: They do indeed afflict us in different ways. Again, it's quite unconscious until you catch it. The problem is that we're complex. We aren't simple, trainlike mechanisms that you can put on a track and let it proceed in one direction. In the course of our lives, we of course have to choose a direction. Are we going to be an athlete, or are we going to be a scholar, or are we going to be a BTS singer or a movie star? The effect is that other things are left behind. Now, it's a good thing that we do that, because then we develop our superior function, and our *ego* development can be fostered and strengthened.

But the problem is that what we leave behind doesn't just go away. It stays frozen in place and often festers, and it becomes like this left-handed little boy who may be unhappy, unruly, and disruptive. We may fall into bad moods, exhaustion, burnout, and various kinds of unhappiness, depression, and anxieties as a consequence of this one-sided development. Those are signals that something is amiss.

Len Cruz: You've pointed out that we leave many things behind. Is it accurate to think that the ones that afflict us were part of our authentic self?

Murray Stein: Yes. They all belong to the self in some way. You're loaded with all kinds of potentials and possibilities. You can't possibly link them all. But some are, let's say, more active and want more attention and need more attention than others.

A lot of people, for instance, in their later years will pick up interests that they left behind in earlier years. That's very good for them psychologically. I know a man who started playing cello in his 60s and discovered that he had a great gift. This was not allowed and not nurtured in his childhood. He had to choose another path in life, but once he got onto that musical path, he discovered a great talent in himself, and it's very meaningful to him to play the cello now. Had he not done that, he would be very unhappy in his later years and probably very envious of other people. In fact, he is one of the least envious people I know.

We come back to the topic of envy. We tend to envy people who are doing things we want to do or who have things we want but don't allow ourselves. So we envy them. However, it's very possible that we are unconscious that we envy them. We just feel unhappy when we see or think about them.

Envy is a signal of something you don't have that you would like to have but don't seem to be able to get your hands on. Sometimes you may not be in fact able to obtain exactly what you envy—for example becoming a star baseball player or a professional musician—but you may be able to attain a satisfactory level of involvement if you give it some time and energy. The man whose inner child wanted to be an artist did not become a Picasso, but he did enough art to satisfy his desire.

Len Cruz: We all have experienced conscious envy; how can we can bring to light unconscious envy?

Murray Stein: That's very difficult. If you're unconsciously envious of somebody, you probably are very critical of them for having what they have and doing what they do. Unconscious envy isn't like a feeling of, "Oh, I wish I had that." It's more like a hatred for the one who has what you envy but can't let yourself admit it.

Len Cruz: With conscious envy we covet what the other has; whereas with unconscious envy, is it more likely that we may want to destroy or disparage what the other person has?

Murray Stein: That's a good way to distinguish between the two. Coveting means you feel you want it. Covet your neighbor's wife: "I wish I had a beautiful wife like that." That's David's story with Bathsheba. And then he gets what he wants, but he commits a terrible act, namely murder of her husband, to get her. He pays dearly for that and confesses his guilt for the rest of his life. But unconscious envy is, as you say, that you want to destroy the other person who possesses it and that's it. For instance, people who unconsciously envy wealthy people, if you ask them, "What's going on? Why are you so critical of that person?" They'll never say, "I wish I had what they have." They'll say, "Well, I don't want to be rich myself, but look at what they're doing with their money, look at how badly they treat other people. They should be taxed. We should take confiscate their money. They should be punished."

Punishment is the thing. That's enough. That's unconscious envy. Now, if you can say, "Wow, I wish I had a billion dollars, and here's what I would do with it," it takes away that edge. You don't want to destroy that person. Maybe you even admire them for the talent they have shown in being about to make so much money.

Unconscious envy is destructive. We see how people can be mobbed, for example on Facebook and other social media platforms. A lot of that is envy driven, and it's extremely destructive.

Mirroring and the Narcissist

Len Cruz: Earlier you mentioned that the mere act of attentive listening on the part of the therapist is one way that a patient can awaken to *shadow* and you've given examples of things people have used to grasp *shadow*. How else does the analyst, the Jungian analyst specifically, engage *shadow* material when working with a patient?

Murray Stein: It really depends a lot on the patient and the patient's ability to look in the mirror. If you're working with a patient who is quite narcissistic or is very sensitive to criticism for whatever reason, maybe from their past traumas, you have to be very careful about approaching the *shadow*.

You practice what von Franz called "bush politics" with the *shadow*. In other words, von Franz said if you approach the *shadow*, you must behave as if you are in the bush, in the jungle, approaching a foreign tribe. They don't know who you are. They can't trust you. When they see you, you must wave white flags to let them know you aren't going to hurt them. You have to bring them presents. You have to tell them how wonderful they are. Then they'll let their guard down enough to let you in closer.

With a lot of patients, you have to practice what we call positive mirroring and empathy before you can ever start approaching anything to do with the *shadow*. They will bring *shadow* issues up indirectly, and you can only listen and mirror your support. In time, you can ask a few questions. But if you start looking at them from another perspective, other than their own, and they are very sensitive to criticism and narcissistically vulnerable, you'll make yourself into an enemy. Then they'll see you as one of those people who doesn't like them and who want to destroy them.

Len Cruz: Most people think of a narcissist as being impervious to criticism; after all, they are so self-absorbed. You seem to be suggesting that the narcissist can be profoundly sensitive.

Murray Stein: There are different types of narcissists. I think there is a narcissist who doesn't pay attention to anybody else. This is a defense against being hurt by criticism. It's a thick wall. But there is a type of narcissist who is hypersensitive to criticism, and whenever they receive any, they strike back with intense anger and aggression. We know a few of those in public life.

The reason some narcissists don't pay attention to anybody else is that they can't take it at all. They just seal themselves off from any outside perspective, because they can't bear the slightest hint of another perspective. So when working with *shadow* material in analysis, the analyst generally will be very careful and alert for instances where the *shadow* is appearing and speaking for itself, in a dream, for instance. Just by listening to a patient's story and helping them to overhear themselves a bit will over time improve their ability to reflect on themselves. The problem with narcissism is there's no self-reflection. It's usually empty of self-reflection. The mirror the narcissist looks into shows only positive and ideal features. It does not tell the truth. When it does, there is an outburst of narcissistic rage, as we see in the story of Snow White, for instance. The narcissist is looking in a mirror but seeing only the *persona*.

The analyst sees the positive value of *shadow*. If you can frame *shadow* in a positive way, the narcissist can hear it, and they can do something with it. For example, if a narcissist has a hugely negative reaction to somebody, and they come and they report that to you, that somebody insulted them, or did something hurtful to them, and they had a huge reaction against that, you can cast that reaction in a way that makes them feel OK about it but helps them to reflect on it at the same time. You can say, "You certainly took care of yourself in that situation. You needed to defend yourself!" and that will bring up a moment of reflection, and maybe they'll begin to consider, "Well, I probably didn't need to do it that much."

Len Cruz: If a therapist resonates in a positive fashion to a narcissist in the midst of their self-inflation, does that mean that they'll take sort of a counterpoint?

Murray Stein: That's been my experience. If you mirror it positively, and not critically. Mirroring it critically would be to see it from the other person's perspective. But you're seeing it from their per-spective, and you're heightening the value of it. Then they can bring it down. What you want to do with the *shadow* is bring reflection. You want to bring a person around to seeing that there is an important part of themselves in the *shadow*. It's a valuable part only distorted and disfigured by judgment. The person can then consider that they don't need to enact the *shadow* in the way they had done before but draw something of value from its energies.

Len Cruz: How does fostering a greater awareness of *shadow* change our interpersonal world and our tendency toward conflict and projection?

Murray Stein: I think that it makes us less one-sided and more interesting. A person who isn't aware of their *shadow* gives you a kind of two-dimensional experience. They may be very fascinating or attractive at first, but you very quickly get tired of it because it just repeats itself and it doesn't go anywhere.

If a person is able to see their multidimensionality—let's put it that way—and not hide what are called typically *shadow* aspects, they'll be able to laugh at themselves. They have a better sense of humor, they'll have more depth, and they're less predictable. So, you can have a much more interesting conversation with such a person than you can with a person who is really locked up in the *persona* and is locking out any *shadow* aspects. They're make you uncomfortable because you sense they're hiding an essential part of themselves, their emotional reality.

Collective Unconscious

Len Cruz: You've spoken of the personal unconscious; let's move on to the domain of collective unconscious and how the *shadow* manifests itself within the collective body?

Murray Stein: The collective *shadow* is the sum of many personal *shadows* magnetized in a certain direction. Think of metal filings: You can put the metal filings on a piece of paper, and then you move a magnet underneath the paper, and this makes the filings move in a direction in line with the magnet. In the collective unconscious, there is an *archetypal shadow*; it's innate, inherent, always was and always will be there in the psyche of the group. The archetypal *shadow* collects the personal *shadows* of the group members and moves them in the direction of the magnet. The magnet is the group leader, the Führer, as the Germans call him.

In modern times, the classic example of this phenomenon is what happened in Germany in the 1930s. Within a few years, people were drawn into a political movement that previously had existed only latently but had not been directed forcefully in a particular direction. The collective *shadow* was "constellated," as we say. The leaders collected the resentment and envy that was resident in the national psyche and using the long-standing native anti-Semitism that had been residual in German and European culture for centuries, they found a powerful magnet that could move the individuals like filings on the surface of a piece of paper.

The leaders, especially Adolf Hitler, discovered that by using anti-Semitism, they could mobilize people's emotions, point them in a certain direction of action, and get political benefit from it. Certain political elements in the United States of America have done the same thing with racism. There are residual strains of racism that can stir emotions like fear and hatred and be directed in certain directions for political gain. You can see that working in the country today.

The unconscious racism, which is a part of the collective *shadow* in the country, can be stimulated and activated and used politically, and people very naively thinking they're not racist will vote for a racist, because they are racist unconsciously. In the collective, the *shadow* activity becomes very dynamic, because many people are participating in it, giving energy to it, consciously or unconsciously.

Len Cruz: What would name that current in the generic. I know that you can give examples.

Murray Stein: In the generic, it's evil. At the bottom, *shadow* is evil, it's the will to destroy. And it's a very clever character. The devil is a very clever crafty fellow, and he captures us. In the Bible, the first incidence of serious *shadow* activity is murder, when Cain kills his brother, Abel. Cain gets very angry because Abel's offering is preferred by God. His offering is accepted, and Cain's offering is not accepted, so he gets very angry at his brother. God comes to him and says, "Cain, you're very angry. Be careful. Sin is lying at the flap of your tent." He adds: "Evil is lying at the door. But you can manage it." But when Cain goes out of his tent, the *shadow* gets him, and he takes his brother into the fields and murders him. That thing that's lying at the flap of the tent is archetypal evil. It's at the core of the *shadow*—in the collective, and in the individual—and it collects emotions like resentment and envy, pride and lust and all the other destructive emotions around it. If we fall into its grip, we become it, even if only momentarily. We become possessed, and this can happen to individuals and to nations. Once it becomes tribal, it's very hard for the individual to resist its intoxicating effect. Evil lurks in the collective unconscious, and you can easily succumb to it.

You often succumb to it before you know it. Your emotions take you there. I'm talking about the way in which people are like the metal filings and can be magnetized, galvanized into a certain direction. It's emotional. It's mob psychology. Emotion captures people and takes them where it wills. So, we see these rallies where people are shouting and screaming, and they're largely unconscious of what they are participating in. When you take an individual aside and quietly ask them what they are shouting about and enthusiastically supporting, they often don't know. People at this level are like animals participating in a collective emotional situation, and the politicians cleverly use them.

Len Cruz: Without diminishing the gravity and the horror of racism or the Holocaust, can we also say that people can become possessed by a similar collective passion with noble rather than evil roots, for example, Gandhi's march across India or the civil rights movement in the 1960s in the U.S.A.?

Murray Stein: Yes, you can say that good can also mobilize in a similar way. We become possessed by ideals and basically noble values. We don't just have bad archetypes; we also have good ones. We have the savior, we have very light and noble Ideas. Justice is one. There are gods and goddesses of justice, weighing the scales. Justice and compassion. And we have symbols of justice like the Statue of Liberty, which are capable of galvanizing us with our noble thoughts and motives, and people will sacrifice themselves for that. People can be magnetized to make great and noble sacrifices for the good just as unconsciously as people can be galvanized unconsciously to rape and murder.

Len Cruz: So, is this magnetic force the archetype?

Murray Stein: Yes. The archetype is the magnet, and it's a question of who moves the magnet and where. As in the individual psyche, certain memories and experiences cluster around archetypal cores and form complexes the same thing happens at the level of the collective psyche. You have these magnets at the bottom of the collective unconscious, and material gathers around the magnets, and individuals are drawn into or captured by them. Then they can be manipulated. The force that draws and holds the filings together is emotion. For instance, if you have strong feelings of a need for revenge, as the Germans had after the First World War, and you locate the enemy—in this case it's the Jewish people—the emotions gathered around the need for revenge, even the idea of justice, can get drawn into this vortex in a perverted way.

People at the collective level begin to think, "We're going to eliminate this cancer from the body politic." This feels like a good and noble thing to do for the collective. The emotion behind this is intense, and some people will feel very noble about carrying out violent and destructive actions even to the point of self-sacrifice. Religious zealots do the same thing. In the name of the good, they fall in the hands of the evil that waits at the flap of the tent.

In one of his last works he wrote, Jung discussed the subject of conscience. Conscience is usually taken to be that inner voice that tells us what is right and what is wrong. Jung says, however, that there is a good conscience and there is a false conscience. Sometimes our conscience misleads us into doing terrible things. We're doing them for a noble reason, but they're terrible things that we're doing. It's very difficult to sort out whom we're following, and for what reason.

Len Cruz: Strangely, the person caught up in either of those, the great movements that are inspired by noble conscience, or the ones by bad conscience, are being lifted up into something that's greater than their individual lives. That can be very validating.

Murray Stein: It is really a matter of emotion taking charge of the collective psyche or the individual psyche. Emotion takes over, and, yes, it's very validating. When you look at this consciously, rationally, and coolly, however, and begin to analyze the situation, you might see it very differently. You might see that you were inflated, intoxicated, really out of yourself. And now are engaged by a very different part of the psyche: your reason. You're using your cognitive functions, the part of the *ego* that is capable of stepping back from emotion and looking at its sources and analyzing them. This is what ethical thinkers do, actually. They are not gripped by emotion. They are very rational even if their ultimate values are grounded in feeling or religion.

So, in this mode we might ask: Where does this strong emotion come from? And if you can do that, then we can make a conscious choice about what political or collective movements to give our energy to. You can participate in a great collective movement but not do so as a part of the mob. Instead, you can do it for conscious reasons. A person might think, "I'll do it because I've thought it through, and I can agree with the principles and I can agree with the direction." We hope the courts and the justice system will operate that way, from a principled position and not from an emotional political position.

BTS *and* Celebrity

Len Cruz: A person who has the ability to mobilize and magnetize people assumes a high responsibility. What do you make of the recent surge of interest in your writings, and in Jungian psychology in general, encouraged by BTS. That musical group's ability to magnetize people has been turned to a very good purpose, toward noble ideas. What are your impressions of this phenomenon, of fandom in general, of a celebrity's responsibility, and the politics of the moment?

Murray Stein: I can tell you that what impressed me about BTS was a talk that RM (a member of BTS) gave before the United Nations. This was a year or two ago. In the talk, he spoke about himself. He said, "As a group, and as individuals, we've achieved great celebrity and fame. But I know I'm not that person who is the celebrity. I come from a small village, quite a ways from Seoul, the capital, and I remember my roots. I remember who I am. I remember where I came from."

That reassured me that the leader of this group has maintained a sense of himself, apart from his hugely celebrated *persona*, and not fallen victim to the seductions of fame. He is a very gifted dancer, singer, rapper, and performer. I hope that all the members of the group stay similarly close to themselves. If they do, it might prevent them from being used up by powerful forces for ulterior motives, such as political motives, or financial motives, or some other less noble purposes. Their message is a good one, it's useful, and it's critically important for the young fans who follow them. If the fans really get the message, and not simply fall into the glamour of it all, they can benefit from BTS.

People are making money and gaining power from the fame and popularity of this group, however. I hope that BTS will manage to continue to be aligned in a direction of wholesome awareness, consciousness, development, and balance. This is what they're putting forward in their message of psychological maturity and development, which we call individuation.

When they pick up on *persona*, and now make an album on *shadow* and *ego*, these are opportunities for their fans to learn some psychological lessons. Of course, they are mesmerized and magnetized by the group and might do almost anything for them. It really is a mob psychology at the concerts. But it is also an opportunity for their fans to be exposed to a message of psychological value that will deepen them, some of them at least.

We can imagine that some BTS fans may start asking, "Well, what's the meaning of these lyrics? What are these symbols all about? What are they saying?" I've tried to interpret that a bit with the first album in *Map of the Soul: Persona, Our Many Selves*. When BTS comes out with their new album on *Shadow* and *Ego*, it will be interesting to explore those lyrics as well.

I'm very curious to know what will be their message about *shadow* and what impact this will have on their fan base. Will it help their fans to begin looking behind their backs, reflecting on themselves a little bit, asking their neighbors to give them an objective view of themselves? That would be great— people becoming more conscious at that age. Their fans are mostly young people, teenagers, or people in their early 20s.

Len Cruz: What a great model of responsible celebrity BTS may be offering. If you attain that kind of celebrity, the chances are that you can't avoid influencing your fan base for better or for worse.

Murray Stein: Celebrity brings a level of responsibility to BTS that I doubt they ever anticipated when they started out singing and dancing as young boys. My impression is that some of them at least are aware of that, and they want to do the right thing. They show themselves as serious and demonstrate to their fans the value of striving for psychological maturity.

Len Cruz: Do you think there's anything specific to Korean culture that contributes what we are seeing manifest?

Murray Stein: I don't know. I've been to South Korea a few times, to Seoul, and I have some friends there. They are rooted in a very traditional Confucian and Buddhist culture, although I think over half of South Korea is now Christian. It tends to be a very conservative culture. These BTS performers, however, don't look very conservative, with the color of their hair and their body movements. I think they're trying to break out of a traditional culture and show another way, something more international.

In traditional cultures, people tend to get trapped in age-old habits of behavior and attitude, and individuals are not much valued. I think BTS is helping in the modernizing of Korean culture, in the sense that individuals will be more valued for their various gifts and qualities. BTS encourages people to develop themselves more as individuals than just as members of a society or as part of a collective.

Len Cruz: Is there anything else you can share with the reader about *shadow*?

Murray Stein: What has been very helpful for me, personally, has been that awareness of *shadow* make one humble. It makes you human. My best helpers, in this regard, have been very dear friends, my wife, and colleagues who can express and show me my failings and my *shadow* side. It is human nature to be something of a know-it-all who thinks, "I know better and I've got the answers." These people show me the mistakes I make in a humorous way, with laughter, and that lightens the load considerably. If it's not a dire and dreadful accusation, but a story told with a sense of humor, you can laugh at yourself, also, and you can start watching yourself in a friendlier way than you might when you feel too accused and too guilty about *shadow* enactments.

Len Cruz: This reminds me of the biblical principle captured in the idea "you shall know them by their fruits." People who undertake the difficult work of engaging their *shadow*, becoming more conscious of it, will be recognizable by their fruits of humility, humor, and charity toward others.

Murray Stein: I think that's a very good place to conclude our conversation.

Chapter 5
The *Shadow* and the Problem of Violence
By Murray Stein

What causes people to commit acts of violence? Violence stalks us like a lurking shadow. It is critically important to understand the source of violence among human beings—for individuals, for societies and for international relations. This has always been a topic crying out for explanation, and today it is especially essential to understand this *shadow* feature of human behavior if we are to make any headway at all in slowing down the rampant proliferation of violence. Violence is spreading through the world like a wildfire, and we ask: Why? Why is this *shadow* so active today? What causes these eruptions of violence on every side? Nearly everywhere we look or whatever we read in the media relates to the subject of violence: brutal aggression in sexual relations, random shootings in schools and other public locations, bullying in the social media, nuclear threats between nations—this list could be extended on and on. What is the source of all this violence? What motivates its outbreak in individuals and societies? If we can discover that, then maybe we can do something to dampen and contain it.

I approach this topic as a Jungian psychoanalyst and will conduct the search by looking into the psychological motivations that lead to violent actions. I begin by considering a story from the book of *Genesis* in the Bible. There we read about an episode of extreme violence at the very beginning of history. This is a mythical story that puts violence into a psychological context and gives us an insight into its motivation.

And the human knew Eve his woman, and she conceived and bore Cain, and she said, "I have got me a man with the Lord." And she bore as well his brother, Abel, and Abel became a herder of sheep while Cain became a tiller of the soil. And it happened in the course of time that Cain brought forth from the fruit of the soil an offering to the Lord. And Abel too had brought from the choice firstlings of his flock, and the Lord regarded Abel and his offering but he did not regard Cain and his offering, and Cain was very incensed, and his face fell. And the Lord said to Cain.

"Why are you incensed,
 and why has your face fallen?
For whether you offer well,
 or whether you do not,

at the tent flap sin crouches
and for you is its longing
but you will rule over it."

And Cain said to Abel his brother, "Let us go out to the field." And when they were in the field, Cain rose against Abel his brother and killed him. And the Lord said to Cain, "Where is Abel your brother?" And he said, "I do not know. Am I my brother's keeper?" And He said, "What have you done? Listen! your brother's blood cries out to me from the soil. And so cursed shall you be by the soil that gaped with its mouth to take your brother's blood from your hand. If you till the soil, it will no longer give you its strength. A restless wanderer shall you be on the earth." And Cain said to the Lord, "My punishment is too great to bear. Now that you have driven me this day from the soil and I must hide from Your presence, I shall be a restless wanderer on the earth and whoever finds me will kill me." And the Lord said to him, "Therefore whoever kills Cain shall suffer sevenfold vengeance." And the Lord set a mark upon Cain so that whoever found him would not slay him.[1]

---

[1] Genesis 4: 1-13. Quotation from *The Hebrew Bible*, Volume 1, translation by Robert Alter, W.W. Norton, 2019.

Myths tell us general human truths, and this one gives us a fundamental insight into the psychological source of violence.

I recently heard a talk in Zurich given by a colleague, Dr. Marco Della Chiesa, who discussed two German words, *würdigen* and *entwürdigen*, and listening to him, I related his insights to the problem of violence and its source. *Würdigen* means to value someone or something, to bestow worth; *entwürdigen* means the opposite—to take worth away, to devalue. These verbs can also be translated as "to respect" and "to disrespect." In the biblical story we read that the Lord found Abel's offering worthy: It was valued. The offering of his elder brother, Cain, on the other hand, he found unworthy: It was devalued. And this judgment produced an emotional reaction in Cain that resulted in violence. Cain felt devalued (*entwürdigt*) and, as a consequence, he murdered his brother.

The story of Cain and Abel turns on the issue of feeling valued and respected or rejected and devalued. To be devalued is humiliating. When the Lord sees Cain's emotional reaction to His rejection of the offering he brought, he warns him that "at the tent flap sin crouches." This is a vivid image: "sin" is an animal waiting at the edge of consciousness and ready to spring. "Sin" means the power of evil, the *shadow*. The *shadow* is waiting to take him in its claws and prepare him to commit an act of extreme violence, murder. The *shadow* will be pleased to shed his brother's blood.

And Cain immediately falls victim to this *shadow* of violence. The Lord's cautionary warning does not restrain him. Psychologically, we would say that he has a weak conscience. Nor does he think ahead of consequences if he acts on his violent impulse. Straightaway, he invites his brother to take a walk out into the desert, then turns on him and without explanation kills him. This murderous act results from a combination of a) his reaction to the Lord's rejection of his offering (*Entwürdigung*), b) his lack of attention to his conscience as represented by the Lord and his failure to consider long-term consequences of his behavior, and c) being taken over and possessed by the *shadow* ("sin"). Violence issues from this toxic mixture of humiliation, *ego* weakness, and the power of the *shadow*.

I will reflect in turn on these three factors and then offer a formula for predicting acts of violence.

First, the *shadow*. This biblical picture of Sin waiting at the fringe of consciousness to pounce is instructive. We often tend to take the *shadow* lightly as some kind of minor character flaw or a slightly hidden motivation, and do not grant it the archetypal energetic power it really possesses. It is, as we know from psychology, an archetypal power and something within us, always there potentially in all of us. Jung tells us that the idea

> … that the soul is empty, and must therefore be filled from without, is still widely, and alarmingly, prevalent nowadays. That

is why people are still convinced of their own complete harmlessness, although they couldn't be further from the truth. This idea of being harmless has to do with the idea of the alleged emptiness of the soul: If anything evil can be found in it, it must have entered it from the outside! Therefore, someone else must be immediately held responsible for this, be it their father, mother, or schoolteacher. But the soul is not a *tabula rasa*, it is already filled with good and evil when we come into the world. As a matter of fact, there are all kinds of things in it, though we may remain unconscious of this.[2]

Naively, we project the *shadow* outward and assign blame for our behavior onto familial, social or political forces outside of ourselves. We want to say, "It's my mother's fault that I did it," or "It's society's fault that I commit acts of violence." These may be contributing factors, but they are not the whole story. Generally, people feel they are innocent and victims of others. It they commit an act of violence, "It's somebody else's fault and not mine, because I couldn't possibly do such a thing on my own inner motivation." But, in reality, the source is inside the psyche and hidden in the unconscious. The motivations for good and evil are powers within the soul that can drive us to take action on their behalf.

---

[2] C.G. Jung, *History of Modern Psychology*, Vol. 1, pp. 22 and 23.

Jung would speak of the *shadow* as the dark side of the self and thus a part of everybody's personality.

In the biblical passage, the Lord tells Cain that he will rule over the power of the *shadow*. In this case, He is mistaken. For Cain, the *shadow* was overpowering, and his *ego* was too weak to resist it. Yet, the Lord's words do give us assurance that we don't necessarily and inevitably have to fall victim to violent, destructive impulses. The human subject is not helplessly at the mercy of the *shadow*. Cain does not use whatever potential he may have to resist evil, but it is there, and most people actually manage to draw on this strength to refrain from acting out violently when disrespected and humiliated. What makes the difference between the people who do and those who don't fall totally into the clutches of the *shadow*? This is an important question for psychotherapists, as it is also for teachers, parents, and indeed for all of us. It is a question I will come back to a bit later.

Second, I will consider the "trigger" that leads to violence. Cain was triggered by feeling unaccepted, unvalued, and unworthy when the Lord did not respect his sacrifice. His brother's offering was deemed worthy and acceptable, but his was not. This was what made Cain's face fall, induced rage, and led him to fall in with the *shadow* of violence. We see that disrespect (*Entwürdigung*) is the trigger.

Francis Fukuyama, the political and economic scientist who became famous some years ago for his book *The End of History and the Last Man* has recently restated some of his views in a new work, *Identity: Contemporary Identity Politics and the Struggle for Recognition*. In it, he suggests a basic reason for why *Entwürdigung* is such a sensitive trigger:

> To be poor is to be invisible to your fellow human beings, and the indignity of invisibility is often worse than the lack of resources. ... Economists assume that human beings are motivated by what they label "preferences" or "utilities," desires for material resources or goods. But they forget about thymos, the part of the soul that desires recognition by others, either as isothymia, recognition as equal in the dignity to others, or megalothymia, recognition as superior. A great deal of what we conventionally take to be economic motivation driven by material needs or desires is in fact a thymotic desire for recognition of one's dignity or status.[3]

Thymos is a Greek word more or less equivalent to *Würdigung*. One of the essential needs we have as human beings, Fukuyama argues, is to be recognized by others, either as an equal or as someone superior who belongs to an elite. If this fails to occur, we risk being triggered to resort to acts of violence. This was

---

[3] Francis Fukuyama, *Identity: Contemporary Identity Politics and the Struggle for Recognition*, pp 80 – 81.

precisely what happened to Cain. We tend out of cultural habit to attribute violence in our society to poverty, poor parenting, lack of education, etc. While these factors may play a subsidiary role, at a deeper psychological level the lack of recognition and respect (*thymos* or *Würdigung*) is often what really drives people to acts of violence.

My wife told me some years ago of a lecture she heard by a well-known research psychologist who had interviewed a large number of prison inmates who had been convicted of violent crimes, mostly of murder. These were considered to be hardened criminals, exceptionally violent people. He asked them the basic question: What caused you to commit murder? Why did they kill the wife or the brother or the stranger on the street? The most frequent answer to that question, he reported, was: "I was 'dissed.'" This is a street word for "disrespected." The withholding of *thymos* (*Entwürdigung*) can beget a very dangerous situation and result in violence, depending on who is being disrespected.

Fukuyama expands on the significance of the assignment or withholding of *thymos* in a highly suggestive way that has a bearing on our topic of the *shadow* of violence in our time particularly. He notes that the ancient Greeks granted special *thymos* to the military heroes who had defended their cities. The heroes were most highly valued and recognized as an elite, as *aristos*. They were given the honor of being named aristocrats, and they received the greatest degree of *thymos*, the highest regard. Over time a

hereditary aristocracy grew up from their descendants, and for a time at least, the rest of the
population felt content to live without that type of
thymos and didn't consider it amiss that this honor
was only granted to the great heroes and their
descendants. But over time and through demo-
cratization and the evolution of consciousness in
Western cultures, so-called commoners also began
demanding a greater degree of *thymos*. Today this has
been woven into our understanding of human rights:
Every human being should be granted respect for the
simple reason that they are human. That doesn't
mean everybody is equal in all respects, but it does
mean that we should give everyone equal respect as
a human being. Christianity also played a role in this
since it taught that everybody has an immortal soul,
that everybody can be saved if they believe in Christ,
and that everybody can go to heaven if they conduct
themselves well and receive the grace of God. Every
soul thus became equal in God's eyes.

This notion of *thymos* for everyone has been
woven into our collective consciousness so that if
anyone is disrespected or humiliated, they're liable to
have a powerful negative reaction, to feel frustration,
anger, and very disagreeable emotions. These
emotions can burst into flame and be taken up by the
shadow and from there led to extreme violence.

In an article titled "The affective basis of
violence" Richard Mizen argues that violence is
fundamentally psychological and is based on emotions.
Emotions are complex collections of chemical and

neuronal responses that form a pattern. If the patterns have a traumatic core, we call them *complexes*. When activated by an event, complexes develop into energetically charged fields that break into consciousness as strong feelings. At first, the stimulated complex is unconscious. It begins by stirring the gut or the sweat glands and then it enters into consciousness as a feeling. Negative feelings cause suffering, anguish, or frustration and can steer one toward violence.

Violence is essentially a psychologically driven phenomenon. It results from the failure to metabolize or contain unbearable feelings. This is what happened to Cain: He experienced an unbearable feeling of rejection and couldn't contain it, even though the Lord assured him he could master it. Because he couldn't contain it, process it, metabolize it, and transform it into thoughts and words, he fell into the hands of the *shadow* of violence.

Jungian psychoanalyst Astrid Berg, in reviewing Mizen's article, suggests that there is a still a deeper layer to this overflow of negative feelings resulting in violence, namely "what for Jung lies in the depth of the human *shadow*, namely archetypal evil, 'the dark God... [who] has slipped the atom bomb and chemical weapons into [our] hands.'"[4] The *dark god* is what is lying in wait in the *shadow*.

---

[4] Astrid Berg, *Journal of Analytical Psychology*, 64:4, p. 634, quoting Jung, *CW* 11, par. 747.

This is the psychological background for acts of violence: Feelings of humiliation and devaluation lead to rage, and these impact the subject in such a way that the *shadow* of violence becomes a handy option and may take control.

From these three factors we can construct a formula that will predict the probability of violence:

$$(D \times F) + (E \times N) \times S = Risk\ of\ Violence$$

In the first part of this formula, *D* stands for disrespect and is a constant, with the value of "1." *F* is the intensity of feeling aroused by an act of disrespect and is rated on a scale of "1" to "10." Some acts of disrespect are relatively small objectively, but they can be perceived as very large subjectively. It's the perception of disrespect (*D*) that counts. The number assigned to *F* depends on how would the subject ranks the feeling of disrespect on a scale of "1" to "5." If it's a "5," it's very high and will generate strong emotions. This part of the formula indicates the intensity of the feeling stimulated by an act of disrespect. In Cain's case, the level of sensitivity to disrespect was high, a "5."

The second part of the formula relates to *ego* deficits. *E* stands for the *ego* and is a constant with the value of "1." *N* refers to the degree of *ego* deficits on a scale of "1" to "5." If the subject has *ego* deficits at a high level, it means that the subject cannot contain much emotion. If the *ego* deficits are at a low level, the subject can contain a lot more negative emotion. A "strong *ego*" means a person has a strong capacity for containment of emotion and the ability to metabolize emotions and transform them into feelings that can be expressed in a symbolic way, as by language. A strong *ego* is also able to consider ethical issues and to reflect on consequences of behavior in the future. In Cain's case, the *ego* is childish and suffering from major deficits, so is obviously rated a "5."

The S in the formula represents the archetypal *shadow* and can have a value as low as "1" or as high as "10," depending upon psychic circumstances and constellation. In some people, it is more strongly constellated and present, in others less so. The reasons for this are various. In part, this may have to do with neurological structures in the brain. Studies have shown that statistically violence runs high in some family histories and is therefore considered in part to be a genetical inheritance. Other contributing factors are culture and collective influence. If one lives in a violent tribe or society, the value of S is increased significantly. National and cultural history can raise or lower the S factor in value. Taken together, a neurological disposition and cultural influence can elevate S to a level of "10." This factor can be estimated by the record of violent behavior in the past of the individual.

If there is a high level of perceived disrespect and humiliation ("5"), plus a high level of *ego* deficits ("5"), times a strongly constellated archetypal *shadow* of violence in the unconscious ("10"), one can be 100% certain there's going to be extreme violence. It could be violence directed toward others in the form of homicide or terrorist violence, or against the self in the form of suicide.

I will offer an example of how this formula might be used to capture the complexity of a real-life event and help to understand an outburst of violence. A story about a sudden and unexpecting shooting appeared in the news in December 2019.[5] A Saudi Arabian Air Force trainee at a military base in Florida opened fire on his classmates, killing three of them. As the story unfolded in the news, we learned that he had complained about an incident of disrespect months earlier. An instructor had made fun of his mustache in front of his classmates by referring to him as "Porn Stash," a humiliating moniker that referred to the looks of some well-known pornography actors. "I was infuriated as to why he would say that in front of the class," he wrote in his complaint.[6] This was the insult that brought his emotions into play and created a strong feeling of humiliation in front of his fellow students. In the formula, this would rate a "5" —in the formula, $(1 \times 5) + (E \times N) \times S = $ Risk of Violence.

About the young man we know little except that he was intelligent, a good student, and a person who was generally quiet and kept to himself. We do not have much information about him on which to base an estimate of his *ego* strengths and weaknesses.

---

[5] https://www.washingtonpost.com/national-security/gunman-behavi_-say
[6] https://www.bbc.com/news/world-us-canada-50695766.

From the reported behavioral reactions to the event of insult and disrespect, however, we could presume that his capacities for containment of strong emotions were not very great. Several days before the shooting, it was reported that he had been showing films of other mass shootings to some of his classmates, and his demeanor was observed to be quite agitated and enraged. It is not known how long he had been preparing his act of violence or whether or not he was in a highly disturbed mental condition or subject to hallucinations. He was not in treatment for psychological problems at the time so far as has been reported, but his behavioral signals would have been the basis for a psychiatric referral. One can estimate that his *ego* deficits ran quite high, perhaps at the level of an "4" or "5." So, from the formula, we can see that the probability of an act of violence is running quite high: ("1" x "5") + ("1" x "4.5") x S = Risk of Violence.

News reports also revealed that his behavior had changed significantly after returning from a trip back home to Saudi Arabia. His fellow classmates reported that when he came back to the base in Florida, he was showing a lot of anger toward the United States and toward his surroundings in general. In a message to the world that he left on a computer shortly before he began his shooting spree, he declared that he did not hate all Americans but he did hate American policies that supported Israel. We see that hatred, a strong indicator of S, has entered his expressions of feeling. This emotion gave him a strong impetus toward violence. Further, the backing he seems to have received at home in Saudi Arabia from a powerful collective source of grievance would have helped him justify his action in his own mind and make his act of violence look impersonal, even though it is clear that his specific grievance was highly personal stemming from the demeaning insult and disrespect he received from his military instructor. This combination of grievances, personal and collective, activated the *shadow* of violence (S) powerfully and brought him into a state of mind that drove him to perform an act of murderous violence, probably knowing full well that he would die as a result. Which is what happened. He was shot dead by an officer after he had managed to get off a few rounds from his weapon.

Here we can see that the S factor was also highly constellated and was able to take possession of him. The result was an act of murderous and also suicidal violence. In the formula, then: ("1" x "5") + ("1" x "4.5") x ("10") = 95% risk of violence. There was a slight chance he could have been held back had someone intervened in time and talked him down from his elevated state of possession by the *shadow* of violence, but this did not occur.

In considering his action, one can imagine that this young man may have felt that it was worth giving his life in order to take revenge for his humiliation at being disrespected in front of his classmates. He was achieving some degree of retribution for the insult he had suffered from the American instructor and for the humiliation that his countrymen had suffered at the hands of Israel's military actions over the past 70 years.

   There is an ancient law called the *talion law*, which is an instinctive kind of law governing human relations. The *talion law* states that the punishment for a misdeed or a crime must be exactly equivalent to the injury suffered by the victim: "an eye for an eye and a tooth for a tooth." It's a basic rule that if you commit an act of aggression or violence against somebody, that person is going to require that you pay for it with a similar amount of suffering. If you hit somebody in the face, the person will hit you back in the face; if you kill the person's brother, he or she will want to kill you or your brother. In ancient times, this law was explicit and literally executed. In our so-called civilized times, it is often subtler but still active nevertheless. If you do something harmful to somebody—you stab someone in the back in a business situation, for example—you can be sure that that person is going to try to stab you in the back at a later time. If you humiliate your children, they will humiliate you in turn when they get the opportunity, although often in subtle ways. A child feeling disrespected will find a way to put down his parents by scoffing at them or making fun of them behind their backs. Similarly, if you do or say something as a therapist that offends or disrespects your clients, they will repay your disrespect in kind. They will forget to pay an invoice, or they'll come in late to sessions, or they'll say something that insults you in a backhanded way. This is the *talion law*, and often it operates unconsciously. It's basic to human interactions.

Disrespect will be followed by disrespect, humiliation by humiliation.

Other people might not have reacted so strongly to this particular act of disrespect as this Saudi soldier did. Similar insults happen to people, and they shrug them off or are able to joke about them. Experiences of disrespect can have a large range of possible reactions. Road rage is an example of a strong reaction to perceived disrespect on the highway. I saw an incident recently while driving through town: One car pulled out in front of another when it shouldn't have, and suddenly the offended person angrily honked his horn several times at the offender. One doesn't do that in Switzerland. It is not the custom. People don't honk their car horns unless it's an extreme situation, and this wasn't such. You could tell this driver was enraged by that act of disrespect, and he couldn't contain it enough not to show it. This is a small incident, but sometimes road rage becomes violent. Even small acts of disrespect, if they are directed toward somebody with relatively weak *ego* strength and a strongly constellated *shadow* for violence, are going to produce a reaction that may result in extreme violence.

A large percentage of the murders committed are labeled "domestic violence." These acts of extreme violence are often generated by a perception of disrespect for one's boundaries, for one's prerogatives, or one's position in the family. Entire ethical systems have been elaborated to handle this problem of respect within family systems. In ancient China, for example, the Confucian ethic, which was taught throughout the kingdom, was specifically about respect for parents, for older siblings, and for elders. This was put in place to diminish social violence and create harmony within Chinese society. If a leader can instill such a system of respect in the citizenry, the level of violence will be much less. In the Bible, Moses played this role of leadership by delivering the Ten Commandments to the Israelites. These rules governed their relationships with God and with their fellows and reduced violence within their tribes by instilling a teaching of respect for others.

The formula, *(D x F) + (E x N) x S = The Risk of Violence,* suggests some possible strategies for how to reduce the risk of violence. One is to reduce the amount of disrespect in a group or society through education in behavioral standards (moral rules, polite manners, human rights). Another is to nurture strong *egos* in the people through training in methods of good enough parenting and through psychological education in the public schools, as well as through the utilization of psychotherapy when needed. The *shadow* of violence, the *S* factor, can be addressed by religious, cultural, and political leaders to help make people aware of the dangers inherent in the human condition. Together, these would reduce the level of collective violence considerably.

Chapter 6
"Criminals":
The *Shadow* Bearers of Society
By Sarah L. Stein, PhD

Like individuals, societies have a psyche, and with it comes an unconscious *shadow*. How do social systems deal with the *shadow*? As individuals do, they repress incompatible elements from collective consciousness and project the resulting *shadow* onto the "other." Those "others" can be foreigners, or they can be people who are designated "criminals" and put away out of sight in prisons. The criminal population in prisons becomes the bearer of a society's *shadow*. How does society benefit from this? It is "purified" and therefore feels clean and innocent. As *shadow* bearers, criminals become scapegoats who carry the sins of a society on their backs into the wilderness of prison life. This gets rid of them, but it also makes them fascinating.

There is a profound, deep-seated desire in many people to understand criminals and the criminal mind. The *shadow* is a kind of mystery. It calls for investigation and comprehension. In modern times, this drive for knowledge and understanding has been institutionalized in the field of criminology. The term "criminology" was first used in 1885 by the Italian law professor Raffaele Garofalo.[7] In 1934, Edwin Sutherland, who is considered to be the father of American criminology, offered the following definition for the subject: Criminology is "the body of knowledge regarding crime as a social phenomenon. It includes within its scope the process of making laws, of breaking laws, and of reacting toward the breaking of laws. ... The objective of criminology is the development of a body of general and verified principles and of other types of knowledge regarding this process of law, crime, and treatment or prevention."[8] Note that the concept of punishment is not mentioned in Sutherland's definition. Explanations of criminal behavior and the criminal mind have historically not made use of Carl Jung's psychological theory of the *shadow*. Criminologists have tended to assign responsibility to nonpsychological factors such as environment or biology as being responsible for inducing deviant behavior. Recommendations for solving the problem of criminality in society have followed accordingly: Change the system (e.g., eliminate racism, classism, economic deprivation, etc.) or do some genetic engineering. Since neither of these solutions has been successful, the result has been

---

[7] https://us.sagepub.com/sites/default/files/upm-binaries/87029_Chapter_1_Introduction_to_Criminology.pdf
[8] Sutherland, E. and Cressey, *Principles of Criminology*, 6th ed. (1960).

more and more incarceration of criminals with longer and more punishing prison sentences. The main solution for the problem of criminality has been "lock them up." The net result has been a huge and disproportionate increase in prison populations as the general population has grown.

If we wish to take a different approach, we might consider Jung's theory of the *shadow*. Jung posited that a *shadow* self exists within all individuals and, by extension, in all collective groups of humans: It is a natural result of psychological development. It is, however, counterproductive, and indeed dangerous, to repress the *shadow* permanently. Another way must be found to deal with it. After all, it belongs to the "whole person" and should not be permanently lost. The danger that ensues when the *shadow* is not recognized, made conscious, and understood is that it becomes increasingly toxic. The contaminants leak out into the environment and poison self and others, destroying links between the severed parts and creating neurotic symptoms. As for taking steps toward integrating the *shadow* into collective consciousness on the societal level for the sake of psychological health and greater wholeness, it is essential for societies and their justice systems not to cast out the *shadow* bearers into the wilderness of prison life once and for all time, but rather to understand them, to treat them, and if possible to restore them into normal society. Further, there is an opportunity to learn from these offenders in order to perhaps solve past or prevent current crimes. This insight has led to the restorative justice movement.

This would be congruent with Jung's psychological theory.

In 1989, the criminologist John Braithwaite argued that there are basically two models of criminal justice, each leading to importantly different outcomes for victims, offenders, and societies: reintegrative shaming and disintegrative stigmatization.[9] Reintegrative shaming separates the individual from the deviant act—the act is recognized as "evil" or "bad," but the person who carried out the act is not. In this model, the offending individual is sanctioned in some way for the singular deviant act and is then reintroduced into normal society. The disintegrative stigmatization justice model, on the other hand, makes no distinction between the bad deed and the individual. Therefore, the entirety of the individual is stigmatized as bad or evil, and this person is removed from normal society; in essence, banished. Braithwaite argued that the reintegrative shaming model has greater potential for healing all parties involved; the disintegrative stigmatization model only serves to disintegrate a community by permanently labeling an individual as a criminal and banishing him or her from normal society. Braithwaite's theory is somewhat aligned with Jung's theory in that he advocated for the conscious recognition of the *shadow* as a part of an individual, for a community discussion regarding the *shadow* act, for the involvement of the victim(s)

---

[9] Braithwaite, J. (1989). *Crime, Shame, and Justice.* Cambridge University Press.

and perpetrator(s) in these discussions to gain a deeper understanding of the exact nature of the crime and its repercussions, and for a community decision as to the best course of action. From a Jungian perspective, it appears that Braithwaite was arguing for the incorporation of the *shadow* into the collective conscious and, perhaps more importantly, was warning of the disintegrative effects upon society of repression.

The counterargument to Braithwaite's idealistic notion is that not every individual who is convicted of a crime is capable of a meaningful reentry into society. Not every person who has been imprisoned is able to reform in a positive manner. Serial murderers such as Theodore Bundy, certain sexual offenders (typically called "fixated pedophiles" in criminal justice jargon), and terrorists such as Theodore Kaczynski are examples of individuals who would be unacceptably dangerous to others if released into the general population.

The question then arises: What to do with these individuals who have been deemed to be dangerous when they return to society? Actually, they can be quite useful to law enforcement. A quite successful project has been to study these offenders by conducting intensive interviews regarding not only their crimes but their lies. This has served to advance interrogation techniques for investigators. Another type of positive result occurred when Dr. Robert Keppel, an investigator who worked intimately on Theodore Bundy's case, interviewed "Ted" about another series of murders that was occurring in Washington state.

Ted nicknamed this offender "The Riverman," and with Ted's assistance and his wealth of information about deviant behavior, "The Riverman," Gary Ridgway, was captured. He is suspected to have killed over 50 prostitutes[10].

The theory of restorative justice is an attempt to describe a formula for achieving integration of the *shadow* into collective consciousness. For our purposes here, I will focus on the criminal justice system of the United States, as well as its relationship to other justice systems. I have chosen the United States for examination and critique because of its well-established reputation for maintaining the highest prison population of any industrialized nation in the world. It is also where I live, and so I am most familiar with this national system of prisons.

The United States is a unique, formidable, rapidly changing world power that other countries often turn to for guidance on issues relevant to their societies. While some people consider the criminal justice system of the U.S. to be advanced and sophisticated, when examined from a quantitative standpoint, the argument could be made that its criminal justice system is ineffective. N.I.M.B.Y.—Not in My Back Yard—is a phrase that powerfully captures the American attitude toward the *shadow* elements of society. As long as those elements remain out of sight, they can remain out of mind. This is the repression of the

---

[10] Keppel, Robert D. & Birnes, William J. (1995). *The Riverman*. Pocket Books.

shadow at work on a collective level. The current incarceration rate in the U.S. is 724 per 100,000 people. In the United Kingdom, it is 145 per 100,000, which is generally taken to be the average incarceration rate for an industrialized nation. Russia has an incarceration rate of 581 per 100,000. It seems ironic that Russia, a country known for its brutal dictatorship and relentless punishment of political dissidents, has an incarceration rate far lower than the so-called land of the free. How can this be explained? Is the U.S. more repressive of the *shadow* than Russia?

According to the U.S. Bureau of Prisons, the following are the percentages of the prison population according to criminal offense:

- Drug Offenses: 45.3%
- Weapons, Explosives, Arson: 18.8%
- Sex Offenses: 10.1%
- Immigration: 6.3%
- Extortion, Fraud, Bribery: 6.2%
- Burglary, Larceny, Property Offenses: 5.0%
- Robbery: 3.5%
- Homicide, Aggravated Assault, and Kidnapping: 3.2%
- Miscellaneous: .07%
- Courts or Corrections: .04%
- Continuing Criminal Enterprise: .02%
- National Security: The bureau of prisons reports 53 prisoners but a 0.0% representation in the population[11]

---

[11] https://www.bop.gov/about/statistics/statistics_inmate_offenses.jsp

Nearly half of all the prisoners are serving time for drug offenses. While some may argue that combating drug addiction, distribution, and trafficking is a worthy cause, this does not explain the numbers. We have to look for deeper reasons. In the United States, the war on drugs emerged in the 1980s as a carefully disguised attack on minorities and the underprivileged. These are *shadow* bearers to begin with, and, through incarcerations, the stigmatization becomes even stronger. It is in the interest of the powerful and dominant interests of society to put them out of sight. Hence, the strategy of incarceration. Policies such as disparate sentencing were enacted: Sentencing any minority, but primarily African Americans, to a longer prison sentence for small amounts of crack cocaine, for example, was a common practice. This directly contradicted the sentences imposed on the wealthy, and often Caucasian, for the same (or more) amount of powder cocaine—sentences that were often far more lenient than those handed out to their racial counterparts. Crack is the drug of choice of the poor; cocaine is for the wealthy. Mandatory minimum sentences ensured long-term incarceration for the former but not the latter. While some of these policies have been revised, there remains much room for improvement. Such policies serve the purpose of repressing the *shadow* of the American collective, which seems to feel cleansed as a result. No one pays much attention to the huge numbers of people in the prisons of America who are there for minor infractions. They are the *shadow* bearers of American society.

Perhaps, though, the *shadow* is working its way to the surface of the collective conscious. A new method that mimics Braithwaite's ideology of reintegrative shaming is happening around the world. This method focuses on treatment and prevention of future crimes, as opposed to our current system of vengeance and punishment. This is the movement of restorative justice. For those interesting in learning more about their efforts, please visit the following site: https://www.restorativejustice.org. Some of the initiatives put forth by The Centre for Justice & Restoration include an African effort titled The Sycamore Project, which fosters conversations around criminal justice and victim-offender relationships; another is a Community Restorations project, which is an intensive prison-based program that focuses on character development and faith.

It seems that a new generation of thinkers is emerging in the realm of justice who are focused on restorative rather than retributive measures. This generation is in alignment with Jungian theory, which recognizes that there is more to individuals than a *persona* and a *shadow*. The same needs to be recognized on the collective level. Societies need a *persona* just as individuals do, and, like individuals, they also need to deal with the *shadow*. This trend of self-examination and self-acceptance has been power-fully advocated by the sensational breakout K-Pop band BTS and their album, *Map of the Soul: Persona*. Perhaps the members of Gen Z, as they are known, are willing to examine much more than *persona*—

they may also want to tackle the hard issues of the greater true self. The next step on this path will be to confront the *shadow*.

Chapter 7
Heal Yourself, Heal the World
By Leonard Cruz

The *shadow* is an unwelcome inhabitant as far as the ego is concerned. The ego, that conscious domain of our personality responsible for dealing with the outside world, adapts to the requirements of family and society. At the simplest level, ego is identified with the "I" of subjectivity.

A fundamental feature of mental functions is the tendency to divide experience into pairs of opposites. Jung, the founder of the field of Analytical Psychology, identified many fundamental pairs of opposites like *persona* and *shadow*. The *shadow* can only be understood in relation to the parallel structure of the *persona*. These structures are like a Janus face, and though they face in opposite directions they are inextricably connected.

To reach our fullest potential as human beings involves disentangling ourselves from the grip of the *shadow.* The person wishing to grow and realize a fuller, more authentic life will be well-served by becoming acquainted with *shadow.* The *shadow* proves to be one of our most valuable allies, though it starts out looking as an unwanted intruder.

Every person strikes a balance between adapting to the demands of society (which includes parents, teachers, celebrities, religious leaders, and more) and developing aspects of their most authentic self. The person who becomes too accommodating to society's demands risks losing touch with the authentic self. Whereas, a person who ignores or completely disegards society's demands to conform may be cast out and isolated. We are highly social creatures and alienation from society terrifies most people.

One way to think about the *shadow* is that it stores all the things that could not or were not absorbed into the conscious ego. As *persona* gathers to itself the desirable features, the rest coalesces as *shadow.*

Shadow often makes its presence known when it erupts intensely and unpredictably. The degree to which a person over-identifies with the *persona* correlates with the intensity and unpredictability of these reversals and eruptions.

Psychological work can be accomplished through music, art, literature, poetry and dance as *BTS* continues to demonstrate. Their popularity points to their remarkable ability to tap into universal themes dwelling in the collective domain. *BTS'* music inspired this work and we hope this work will inspire *BTS'* fans to explore their own inner life.

Concluding thoughts

The pain we do not deal with we inflict. This seems to be an axiom of the psychological life. A great deal of human suffering can be traced to people's failure to deal with their own pain. It is a motif that reveals itself repeatedly in the human story. Therefore, one lesson you might take away from this book is that if you wish to heal the world, start by healing yourself.

History reveals that tyrants and despots are often forged in a crucible of personal pain, torment, and abuse. Oppressive leaders work out their personal issues at the expense of the people.

We are reminded of Adolf Hitler whose own spectacular inferiority activated a brutal under-current of barbarism with such deep collective roots that an entire nation and people were magnetized in the direction of war. Fidel Castro's biological father initially refused to acknowledge his paternity. Decades later Castro proved to the paternalistic Yankees that Cuba would no longer allow itself to be ignored like a bastard child. When George W. Bush prosecuted war on Iraq, he seemed driven to finish a job he imagined his father had failed to complete. Moreover, it was widely thought that Jeb Bush, not W, was the son best suited to be president. Perhaps W, a recovering alcoholic who craved his father's approval, led our nation into its most pro-tracted war in part because of his own unresolved issues? The point is that these political figures demonstrate that unresolved issues, considered at the collective unconscious level, can wreak havoc on others.

The person who owns their *shadow* has much to offer the world. First, the mere act of reclaiming a previously disowned part of the self is profoundly healing. It is as if by recovering portions of the *shadow* a person is freed from bondage and servitude to *shadow*. Like Jung recognized even when he was quite young, we have two personalities, in the figures of *persona* and *shadow*. The fruit of working on the *shadow* manifests through diminished projection onto others of the unacceptable, rejected elements within our own personality. *Shadow* work cultivates compassion for others. Once we realize that our emotional outbursts and our brutal reversals cause others untold pain and suffering, we become more understanding of others who are in the grip of their own *shadows*. Befriending or at least acquainting oneself with *shadow* makes a person less defensive, more well-rounded, and better prepared to see themselves with humor.

The deeper we go in this process of owning our *shadow* the greater chance we have of recognizing

collective levels of the *shadow*. The collective elements
of the *shadow* exert their influence in very subtle but
powerful ways. It may appear as bias and micro-
aggressions. As people are swept up in the energy,
influence, and magnetism of the collective *shadow*,
large-scale movements may arise. These movements
often take on a malicious, destructive tenor. At this
larger scale, we see that the disowned, rejected
aspects of a collective body (like a nation, a culture,
an ethnic people) play out destructively. The rise of
the Nazi party is among the most poignant examples
of how an entire people were animated, impas-
sioned, and mobilized by deep, unacknowledged
roots. There are countless current examples of
collective *shadow* playing out throughout the world
today. Those who persecute the Rohingya, who
advance white supremacist doctrine, who attack
indigenous people in order to exploit their lands,
typically justify their actions by projecting onto their
victims.

If humanity hopes to put an end to such
persecution and violence, we must learn to engage
shadow, that may be the best hope for suspending
projection onto the other.

In order to own your *shadow* you must culti-
vate a charitable, loving attitude toward yourself and
the things you had previously deemed unacceptable.
Self-love fosters love of the other. The journey of
individuation is universal in many respects but must
be traversed by every individual on their own. It may

be very helpful to set out with a map and we are indebted to Jung for tirelessly devoting so much of his life to fashioning a map based on his explorations with patients and himself. In the end, the only way to know the territory is to travel the landscape ourselves. Even the best map is just a guide for the journey. For the map to prove useful you must take the journey.

Let everyone sweep before his own door,
and the whole world will be clean.
-Goethe

In the psychological realms, owning your *shadow* and recognizing *persona* as nothing more than a mask, is the equivalent of sweeping in front of your psychological door. Owning your *shadow* is preventive medicine, it keeps you from contaminating the world with your unresolved issues. Individuation also inoculates you from some of the hurts inflicted by the person who overly identifies with the *persona*. When we recognize *persona* as a necessary part of the actor's tools, a mask for the outer world, we can step back from overidentification with these outward features. This results in less tendency for the *shadow* to erupt unexpectedly. You will be less prone to lash out from the *shadow*.

The work of owning the *shadow* fortifies a person against the continual onslaught of society. Throughout life the demand to adapt to society's expectations does not stop just because we embark on a path of individuation. Like the Sirens calling to Odysseus, society's beck and call continues throughout life and is an ever-present risk of shipwreck. It falls to every person to chart a course that honors the authentic parts of themselves while simultaneously adapting to society's demands. It is in this tension that life is lived.

Our world is ailing. The environment is under attack and the fragile ecosystems that we depend on to sustain life are in danger. Our collective *persona* glorifies wealth accumulation and consumption, but the collective *shadow* often relies on the exploitation of poor nations and their natural resources to support these passions of the collective *persona*. The wide-spread political divisiveness we observe in Europe and the USA are rooted in factions who overidentify with their collective *persona* and project wildly onto opposing factions the elements of their collective *shadow*. Those who are born (or live) in the northern hemisphere often behave as if the wealth and privilege they enjoy is solely a result of the collective qualities of industrialization, civilization, and culture (collective *persona* identification) and regard those living in the southern hemisphere as less developed, uncivilized, and lacking in high culture (projections of a collective *shadow*). These kinds of splits between *persona* and *shadow* hold enormous potential for continued destructiveness, yet they also provide enormous possibilities for healing. The place to start is always in the tension of our personal *shadow* and *persona*.

"Life's most persistent question is,
what are you doing for others?"
Dr. Martin Luther King, Jr.

Shadow work cultivates greater conscious awareness of the unacceptable, disowned aspects of the SELF. As we become more conscious of *shadow*, projection onto others decreases. The ability to see our own *shadow* qualities cultivates more charity toward others and equips us to recognize projection at the collective level. All these fruits of *shadow* work have the potential to heal the individual and the world at large. It falls to each one of us to do this work for our own benefit and for the benefit of others.

References

Berg, A. (2019). A review of R. Mizen's "The affective basis of violence," in *The Journal of Analytical Psychology*, 64:4, 2019, 632-37.

Fukuyama, F. (2019). *Identity: Contemporary Identity Politics and the Struggle for Recognition*. London: Profile Books.

Jung, C.G. (2009). *The Red Book. Liber Novus.* A Reader's Edition. New York: W.W. Norton.

Jung, C.G. (2019). *History of Modern Psychology*, Vol. 1. Princeton, NJ: Princeton University Press.

Mizen, R. (2019). "The affective basis of violence," in *Infant Mental Health Journal*, 1-14.

About the Contributors

Murray Stein, Ph.D. is a Training and Supervising Analyst at the International School of Analytical Psychology Zurich (ISAP-ZURICH). He was president of the International Association for Analytical Psychology (IAAP) from 2001 to 2004 and President of ISAP-ZURICH from 2008 to 2012. He has lectured internationally and is the author of *In MidLife, Jung's Map of the Soul, Minding the Self, Outside Inside and All Around* and *The Bible as Dream.* The first volume of his *Collected Writings,* titled *Individuation,* has recently been published. He lives in Switzerland and has a private practice in Zurich, Switzerland.

Sarah Stein, Ph.D. is a Cold Case consultant and the co-founder of The Center for the Resolution of Unresolved Crime. She has co-authored two texts on Cold Cases and published several articles related to the topic. Her most recent literary contribution has been a chapter in *Survivors: Shocking True Stories About America's Pursuit of Police Transparency & Justice,* compiled by Dennis N. Griffin of The Transparency Project. She consults and teaches regularly for law enforcement agencies and provides guidance for families regarding unresolved cases in the United States and internationally.

Leonard Cruz, MD is the Editor-in-Chief of Chiron Publications and co-founder of the Asheville Jung Center. He is a contributor to several edited volumes, *The Unconscious Roots of Creativity, A Clear and Present Danger: Narcissism in the Era of President Trump,* and *Map of the Soul – Persona: Our Many Faces* and co-authored *DSM-5 Insanely Simplified.* He currently works in the field of addiction medicine and is exploring the uses of ritual and myth in treatment of substance use disorders.

Steven Buser, MD trained in medicine at Duke University and served 12 years as a physician in the U.S. Air Force. He is a graduate of a two-year Clinical Training Program at the C.G. Jung Institute of Chicago and is the co-founder of the Asheville Jung Center. He has worked for over 30 years in psychiatry with a focus on Jungian oriented psychotherapy. He co-authored *DSM-5 Insanely Simplified* and co-edited *A Clear and Present Danger: Narcissism in the Era of President Trump* as well as *Rocket Man: Nuclear Madness and the Mind of Donald Trump.* He currently works in the field of addiction medicine and serves as Publisher of Chiron Publications.